THE PASSIONATE PERILS OF PUBLISHING
by Celeste West & Valerie Wheat

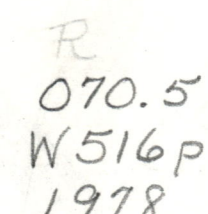

R
070.5
W516p
1978

CONTENTS

Chapter 1	**THE LITERARY-INDUSTRIAL COMPLEX**	1
	Chart: Publishers Owned by Conglomerates	8
	Chart: Publishers' Merger Mania	10
	Notes: Muckraking Madness	12
Chapter 2	**ROLL YR OWN: A Guide For New Publishers, Self-Publishers, and Authors**	15
	General How-To	22
	Design, Graphic Techniques, & Printing	26
	Finishing In The Money	30
	Promotion	32
	Education For Publishing	36
Chapter 3	**DISCOVERING THE WILD & FREE PRESS: Where The Independents Do It & Deal It**	39
	Guides, Directories, Indexes	40
	Alternative Review & News Media	43
	Selected Distributors	46
Chapter 4	**FEMINISTS IN PRINT**	51
	Guides, Directories, Indexes	52
	Selected Feminist Review & News Media	55
	Feminist Book Publishers	57
	Distributors of Feminist Materials	61
Chapter 5	**KIDS' LIBERATED LITERATURE**	65
Chapter 6	**THE LIBRARY FREE PRESS**	69
	INDEX	73

1.
THE LITERARY-INDUSTRIAL COMPLEX
by Celeste West

What do Random House, Knopf, Ballantine Books, Modern Library, Vintage, Pantheon, L. W. Singer, and Beginner Books all have in common? Answer: they are all the same company. These eight houses are the different publishing imprints owned by RCA, the six billion dollar a year conglomerate. A huge defense contractor, RCA also owns NBC, tv and radio stations, markets more than 60,000 products - from Hertz Rent-A-Cars, Banquet Foods, and Coronet Rugs to records and electronic equipment. As the charts on pages 8-9 show, much of the proud publishing industry follows this pattern, control by non-publishing business conglomerates like ITT, Gulf + Western, CBS, Raytheon, Litton, Xerox, etc.

Most people, including even librarians, never notice a book's "brand name" - the publisher. Therefore, unlike the oil or auto industry, concentration of ownership rather than corporate independence is not obvious. *The fact is that a handful of large companies control almost all the books produced in the United States.* According to John Dessauer, the official statistician of the Association of American Publishers, 3.3% of 6000+ publishing companies control 70% of the industry's volume.[1] This high concentration ratio pulls the publishing industry toward "oligopoly," a form of "imperfect" competition where the firms producing and selling books are few in number and large in size.

THE SURGE TO MERGE

Major publishers not yet owned by outside conglomerates seem to be gobbling each other up in a wave of acquisitions which began in the 60's. A typical example is the take-over of Dell by Doubleday ("DoubleDell"), which forms the super-alliance of a major hard cover with a vast mass market paperback line. Favored by publishers because this pattern keeps lucrative paperback reprint rights in house, it is naturally despised by authors whose hardcover publishers once sold rights in a more open market. There were 57 mergers in the printing publishing field in 1977, 58 in 1976, and 47 in 1975, according to W.T. Grimm and Co., a Chicago based merger consulting firm.

Indeed, consolidation seems to be the most remarked upon trend in the book industry today. At the last international book fair in Frankfurt, *Publishers Weekly* said there seemed to be more talk of take-overs than of books. Lawrence Hughes, president of William Morrow & Co. (now owned by the giant *Fortune 500* textbook publisher Scott, Foresman), says the day may arrive in publishing when "instead of 50 major houses, there will be 10 or 15.[2] Dick Snyder, who runs Simon & Schuster for the sprawling conglomerate Gulf + Western, likes the field even narrower:

> *What we're going to see now, if this trend continues, is that like the seven sisters of the oil business we will have seven giant publishing companies of varying size, either as part of a conglomerate or become like a Doubleday, which in itself is a bit of a conglomerate. There will always be room for the dynamic publisher like a Roger Straus, or a Pat Knopf, or people like that. But fundamentally, as in the oil business, they are wildcats....I'm a great believer in the horizontal company, with independent publishing houses being fed into, in effect, one computer, one business department, maybe two sales forces....I would love to see new companies join S & S on that horizontal basis where they keep their publishing integrity but all the accounting and other functions are fed into one operation.*[3]

And the beat goes on. Spokespeople for allied industries like printing and paper manufacturing predict publishers' consolidation will lead to a further consolidation by manufacturers in order to fulfill production requirements.[4]

The marketing of books is also becoming highly centralized, from wholesaler to retail bookstore. The last few years have seen the rise of the "chain bookstore." Walden Book Company and B. Dalton (owned by huge department store chains Carter Hawley Hale and Dayton Hudson respectively) are the giants in this field. They are buying up independent stores and building new ones in seemingly every shopping center. Like fast-food outlets, the chain bookstores are automated for fast, volume turnover of bestseller fare. This new breed of bookseller concentrates on what one of their managers calls "books for non-readers - repair handbooks, cookbooks, and paperbacks that have simultaneous multimedia appeal."[5] The Department of Commerce predicts chains will be doing over half the total bookstore business by 1980.[6] Welcome *Star Wars, Bionic Woman, Jaws* and "the broad band of bland taste." Goodbye specialty books for diverse interests. The national chains' buying clout is immense. They use it to encourage not only "safe," middle-of-the-road purchases, but also to promote their bias for titles like Anita Bryant's hardcover homophobia. At B. Dalton's, *Joy of Lesbian Sex* will not be special ordered for a customer, and *Joy of Sex* is banished under the counter.

CONGLOMERITIS

The conglomerate is a relatively new character in the saga of capitalism. It is simply a container corporation of unrelated businesses amalgamated into a single financial and managerial unit, otherwise known as a "mish-mash."

Conglomerate suitors wooed other media prior to books. They molded the rest of the communications industry into a "mass media" force - selling the greatest number of media units to the most buyers for the highest profit. Diverse, small markets of special information and entertainment exist, but are not served by conglomerate controlled media, whose goal is top dollar. Investments must pay off handsomely to recoup large operating overheads, and make high profits for stockholders and for continued expansion.[7]

As radio, tv, newspapers, records, and movies were commoditized into corporate oligopolies and conglomerates, they virtually abandoned any role in social and cultural leadership.[8] Their owners' overriding concern is cash, not communication. The creative core in each media remains the small, independent producer. However, attempt at media entry by a new company is a capital intensive proposition. You can set up a small, creative (whatever) medium company, but see how much advertising you can afford to spread the word; how much high-powered technology you can buy; and how many theatres, radio station play-lists, tv shows, bookstores, or newstands will open up their air space to you. The independents are simply choked out of expensive distribution channels by the huge conglomerate media flow.

The siren song of conglomerate take-over for publishers is that there will be access to high financing. Publishing has become an inflated, capital intensive business. Trade books are now run on the "star system," with a million dollars not an uncommon sum paid for "properties," later to be hyped with equally lush ad budgets.[9] But what are the social consequences for acquired publishing houses? In publishing, concern with sales has usually been tempered by the independent owner's personal aesthetics and commitments. When a giant corporation steps in, short-term profits are often put ahead of both quality and public service. Can book publishing, the volatile, individualistic profession of ideas, culture, and iconoclasm lose its precious diversity as corporate overlords make "the bottom line" of highest profit the criterion of value?

We know what has happened in other industries. As competitors were acquired, more powerful corporations were created with which the remaining companies had to contend. Few survive, and oligopoly forms, or, in the extreme stage, a monopoly. Many of today's large corporations rose from mergers at the turn of the century. The companies now in virtual control of the auto, oil, tire, steel, copper, tobacco, soap and cereal industries were created during the first great age of "trusts." Two hundred companies now own two-thirds of the manufacturing assets in America, or, put another way, sixty families control half the private wealth.[10] Many people would argue such economic concentration undermines our touted "free enterprise" system. The big fish keep taking bigger bites. Concentration of an industry into a few large companies (oil, drugs, tv, cars, paper, etc.) has historically led to fewer options for the public, less innovation, less competition, and to greater manipulation of the worker and consumer....

Acquired publishing executives stoutly maintain the "gentleman's profession" will not become as crassly commercial as the other media trusts, whose corporate form it is emulating. They say the money men don't even pretend to understand publishing and leave them alone.[11] But we're already getting the circus-like, mass media approach to publishing. Unlike other industries, publishing has been predicated on the gallant accounting system that winners subsidize losers. Bonanza bestsellers or textbooks pay for the belles lettres and non-conformities that usually run red. This is good publishing, but inefficient business. Perhaps kept publishers can take someone else's money and avoid compromising their standards. But whoever holds the purse strings ultimately makes the decision on who gets paid and what gets promoted. Put less delicately, "Fuck with a bull, and you get the horns."[12]

TRUST - BUSTING

Representative Morris Udall included publishing in his Competition Review Act legislation. It is currently before Peter Rodino's House Judiciary Subcommittee on Monopolies, slated for discussion later this year (HR 6098). The Senate Antitrust and Monopoly Subcommittee, chaired by Senator Edward Kennedy, will also be investigating conglomerate takeovers in publishing. Representative Udall argued, in a down-home speech before the Association of American Publishers last year:

Policies and trends in the book industry soon may not reflect the spirit of innovation, creativity and courage that has always been a cherished part of publishing in giving the unknown author a chance. What will be the impact of conglomerate ownership such as CBS owning Holt, Rinehart & Winston and now Fawcett, or RCA's ownership of Random House, or MCA owning G.P. Putnam and Gulf + Western owning Simon & Schuster? Or the newspaper corporations such as the New York Times and Dow Jones and Times Mirror who publish books?[13] Do we really get better books, more chance for unknown authors, or merely more profits for the conglomerates?

...If any industry has a social responsibility, it is the publishers of books. We face the loss of communication and an acute absence of ideas in almost every other media, the principal culprit being concentration and lust for the dollar. Book publishing is a healthy industry. Its receipts were up 7% in 1976 and an anticipated 8% in this year up to $4.1 billion. But earning reports are the siren song of concentration. An industry has the capability of monitoring its own trends and to warn against what may be attractive to the accounts but may be bitter to society. Must we always surrender to a profit? The people of this nation sense the corporate growth to bigness, and similar to their healthy disbelief in the protestations of the oil companies that their profits are not large enough, they may soon tire of the trade publishers spoon-feeding them bestsellers and leaving the fresh and the bold to fend for themselves....

Maybe the obituary for our economic system or a free independent publishing industry may not be on the front page, if that day ever comes. These great central values may just slip away, merger by merger, acquisition by acquisition, stock split by stock split....[14]

AUTHORS' FEARS

The 5000 member Authors Guild has spoken out in alarm, fearing that the 300 publishing mergers and take-overs in the last 20 years are a threat to the quality of American letters. The Guild argues that conglomerates are forcing higher profits through publication of the "surefire seller:" pop books which exploit violence, voyeurism, and personal insecurities. The phenomenon leads to what might be called "Gresham's Law of Publishing:" inferior books drive out good books (and authors.) Mass market shlock may be a cheap read, but it is expensive to grind out. The authors who do celeb books, sensationalism, gothic escape, torrid historicals, and other formulaic genres have hardnosed agents who make publishers pay hugely inflated prices. They literally sell their author to the highest bidder. But conglomerate pockets are deep, and whopping six and seven figure advances are made. Naturally these titles get the lion's share of the house promotional budget. The rest of a publisher's list go out on a wing and a prayer.

Fewer, larger companies diminish the chance of an author's work being bought at all. As previously mentioned, authors can also lose out on lucrative subsidiary rights (paperback, book club, film, tv) if the contracting hardback house makes a sweetheart deal with its own subsidiary - as Doubleday could with Dell, Simon & Schuster with Paramount, *Time's* Little, Brown with Book of the Month Club, etc. The Authors Guild has appealed to the Department of Justice and the Federal Trade Commission to initiate proceedings under the Clayton Antitrust Act to halt this trend. As we go to press, the Justice Department is still investigating the acquisition of Fawcett by CBS and the *Time* take-over of BMOC. In November 1976, the Justice Department did forbid 21 U.S. publishers from conspiring with British publishers to carve up the world market in restraint of trade. This had been going on for 30 years; the FTC and Antitrust section of Justice are not known for quick, decisive moves.

Some writers are also becoming squeamish about conglomerate publishers' tie-in with war games, repressive governments, and the "corporate crimes" a multi-national seems heir to. Would an editor at Bobbs-Merrill (ITT owned) hesitate to accept your manuscript exposing Chilean political torture? If your book earns a profit for Knopf (RCA), will the money be reinvested in RCA military technology? Do you like the fact that Simon & Schuster can run a cheap sales conference in the Dominican Republic because its parent Gulf + Western practically owns the country? If McGraw Hill seems a fond suitor for your feminist book, ask why they fired a highly regarded woman employee for organizing against job discrimination. Their official reason for termination: "obscenity and acts of terrorism."[15]

THE SHREDDER

When huge, sprawling conglomerates are involved, surreal things can happen. We keep waiting for ITT's publishing flock to "bake-a-book." They are giving away aprons at the American Booksellers Association this year. ITT owns extensive timber lands and manufactures "Fresh Horizons" bread, 53% water and wood pulp.[16] Why not print up these slices to capture the legendary "voracious reader?" Then we have Harcourt Brace Jovanovich, lashed into the *Fortune 500* Club by its expansionist president, William Jovanovich. Harcourt owns many, many nonpublishing subsidiaries; its top publishing staff frequently becomes so confused they lose their heads.[17] Last year, however, Harcourt reported a surprising occurrence for a publisher: heavy losses not the result of editorial misfeasance, but due to the death of two killer whales. HBJ owns Seaworld and other "amusements." Luckily, it also owns fifteen fish-and-chips restaurants....

In the area of recycling, it seems amazing that no publishing conglomerate runs a confetti factory. The nightmare of the industry, more especially of authors, is the spectre of "The Shredder." A large percentage of unsold books are returned by bookstores and simply shredded up.[18] There is just so much warehouse space. Many books are yanked off the market like stale bread; shelf life averages 12 days for a mass market paperback, 6 weeks to 6 months for a trade hardback.[19] This is, of course, extremely costly to everyone. In some bookstores, a full-time staff person is necessary for processing returns. The Returns Syndrome is a result of careless overprinting and overhyping a title, with an equally wanton disregard of the editorial material and of the physical resources used. So much for big business efficiency. In setting the cost of a book, publishers figure in statistical return probability, so the consumer actually pays for it all in the end.

SEXISM

Book publishing, like all industries, is controlled by rich, white, heterosexual men.[20] To retain this power, their books naturally reinforce status quo attitudes of privilege and discrimination. The smart publisher will, of course, co-opt any genuine liberation movement that yields short-run profit. Thus, we have been given our dole of dusky faces in the textbooks, clit-lit, and now endless variations on the epic "slave saga."[21] This is at least a change, given a history of outrageously misogynist and racist books, but it's all part of the Wall Street shuffle.

Look at the make-up of the houses themselves. Their labor force is 75-80% white, overeducated, underpaid women.[22] Starting salary last year at Harper was $120 a week.[23] Women are concentrated in the lowest ranks, a few in managerial and sales positions, and virtually none at the top. The anthology, *Rooms With No View: A Woman's Guide to The Man's World of the Media*, edited by Ethel Strainchamps for Media Women's Association (Harper, 1974), includes a devastating section on the blatant and closet chauvinism of book publishers. Sample chapters: "Pride and Prejudice" (W.W. Norton); "The Tender Trap" (Bantam); "Ladies In Waiting" (Lippincott); "Double Duties" (Doubleday): "Caution: Men Working" (Time-Life Books). It took Media Women's Association some pretty rough tricks and two years of haggling to get *Rooms With No View* published. This is the common fate of the uppity book, a pattern documented by June Arnold in "Feminist Presses and Feminist Politics," *Quest*, Summer 1976.

Of course, women are fighting back - most spectacularly in their own publishing ventures (see Chapter 5), but also within the establishment. Sex discrimination suits have just been won against Houghton Mifflin ($750,000) and *Reader's Digest* ($1.5 million.) A discrimination suit is pending against Macmillan. However, attempts to equalize worker power within the industry through union organizing have met with dismal results. Harper & Row and Allyn and Bacon are the only large houses with a union. The trouble comes in organizing an elitist, "glamour" profession, rather than a factory. Employees have a very acute case of "identifying with the oppressor." Author Alice Bach describes the magical spell the publishing world can weave over its foot soldiers in a bitter-sweet piece called "Carrying the Torch for Harper & Row," (*NYTBR* 7/7/74:23). Bach's personal torch began to flicker during the long strike at Harper in 1974; there was another strike in 1977.

The transcendent myth surrounding publishing is certainly waning as the Literary-Industrial Complex tightens up.[24] Editors are cynical. Authors are angry, and readers are bored with pulp and pop. As New York publishing is taken over by a core of merchandisers who simply push "units" from printer to shredder by the fastest route possible - a need for something else is created. It is called the small, alternative, Independent Press.[25] Its seeds really started blowing in the 60's just as old houses began to fall in the merger swath.

It is the slice of tomorrow.

PUBLISHERS OWNED BY CONGLOMERATES

The figure in parenthesis next to a conglomerate name equals total annual sales. It can be seen that IBM, ITT, RCA, and Xerox each take in substantially more than the entire book publishing industry does; total industry revenues were only $4.6 billion in 1977. Publishing is an amazing industry, whose relatively "tiny" revenue is totally disproportionate to its power, influence, and cultural impact. The real return on investment for conglomerates is media clout.

One asterisk by a company's name means it is among *The Fortune 500*, with revenues of $350+ million. Two asterisks denote the company is also listed in *The 100 Largest Defense Contractors* (Department of Defense, 1977.)

Information for these charts was collected, in much flux, from *Publishers Weekly; BP Report: On The Business of Book Publishing; Literary Market Place 1978; Bowker Annual of Library & Book Trade Information 1978; PTLA; Fortune Magazine 5/8/78; Moody's Industrial Manual; Standard & Poor's;* and various annual reports.

The beat goes on . . . .

*ABC ($1.6 billion sales) *TV & radio network; 275 theaters; records; tourist attractions.*
   Magazines (*American West, High Fidelity,*
      Los Angeles, Modern Photography)
   National Insurance Law Service Publications
   Prairie Farmer Publishing Co.
   Schwann Music Publications
   University Park Press
   Word Books (religious books & music)

AMBASSADOR INTERNATIONAL CULTURAL FOUNDATION *Often investigated rich fundamentalist group.*
   Everest House Books
   Quest/78 Magazine

*BELL & HOWELL MICROFORMS ($491.6 million sales) *Business, scientific, & photo equipment.*
   Charles E. Merrill Co.

*CBS ($2.8 billion) *TV & radio network; Columbia, Epic, Odyssey, Portrait Records; Pacific Stereo and Discount Records; Steinway Pianos, Fender Guitars & other instruments; Creative Playthings; films.*
   Crest Books
   Curtis Books
   Editions Doin (French imprint)
   Fawcett (mass market books & 30+ magazines; CBS take-over anti-trust suit pending)
   Gold Medal
   Holt, Reinhart, & Winston
   Magazines (*Woman's Day, Mechanix Illus.,* etc.)
   Movie Book Club
   NEISA (Spanish books)
   Popular Library (mass market pbk)
   Praeger
   W.B. Saunders Professional Books

*CARTER HAWLEY HALE STORES ($1.5 billion sales)
   Walden Book Co. (475 store chain, with approx. $135 million in sales yearly)

*DAYTON HUDSON CORPORATION ($1.9 billion sales)
   B. Dalton Bookstores (298 store chain with $138 million in sales yearly)

DUN & BRADSTREET ($178.5 million) *Business & marketing services; 5 TV sta., sports network.*
   Donnelley Directory (yellow pages publisher)
   Funk & Wagnalls
   Magazines (industrial, travel, medical, trade)
   Moody's Investors Service
   Technical Publishing Co.
   Transportation guides & services

FILMWAYS INC. ($140.6 million) *TV & film production; electronic equipment; studio facilities.*
   Ace Books
   Charter Communications (*Redbook* + fan & confession magazines)
   Cricket Books
   Grosset & Dunlap (Nixonia)
   Ideal Publishing Corporation
   Leads Publishing Co.
   Phi Publishing
   Platt & Munk
   Publishers Distributing Co.
   Tempo

*W.R. GRACE & CO. ($4 billion) *Agri-biz chemicals; natural resources; restaurants & retail stores.*
   Baker & Taylor (largest library wholesaler, now moving into retail; sales $158 million)
   Publisher's Marketing Group

*GULF + WESTERN ($3.6 billion) *Paramount; panty hose; tobacco; sugar; Schrafft's; Madison Square Garden; ammunition; mines; paper; financial services Miss Universe & Miss USA pageants; theaters, including 19 in South Africa.*
   Archway
   Exam Prep
   Fireside
   Julian Messner
   Monarch Press
   Pocket Books, with its imprints:
      Kangaroo (mass market pbk)
      Wallaby (trade pbk)
      Quokkas (classics, rack size)
   Simon & Schuster
   Sovereign
   Summit Books
   Touchstone
   Washington Square Press
   Distributes Playboy Books, Harlequin Romances

HOWARD & WYNDAMS LTD. (British) *Diverse holdings, including Ciro Jewelry, etc.*
   Hawthorne

**IBM ($18.1 billion) *Information handling systems and equipment.*
   Science Research Associates Textbooks

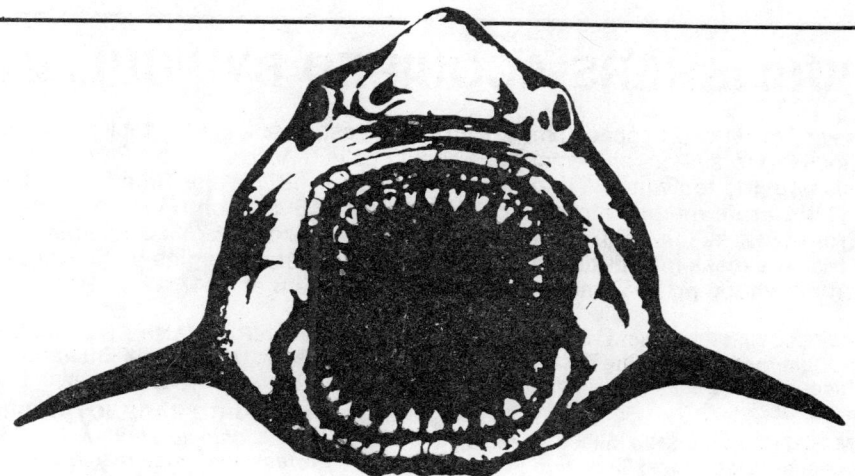

**ITT ($13.1 billion) *Telecommunications; timber; Twinkies; foods; pesticides; paper; business services; mines; Sheraton Hotels; Hartford Insurance; defense/space systems. Can buy up juntas and out of anti-trust suits . . . .*
    Theodore Audel
    Bobbs-Merrill
    Gregg Press
    G.K. Hall Reprint Co.
    Intertec Publishing Co.
    Howard Sams (automotive & electronic books)
    Twayne Publishers
    Who's Who and all Marquise *Who's* directories

**LITTON INDUSTRIES ($3.4 billion) *Electronic equipment & instruments; paper & printing; business products; defense systems & ships.*
    American Book Company
    Delmar Publishers
    Hudson Publishing Co.
    Mason/Charter
    McCormick Mathers
    D. Van Nostrand
    Van Nostrand Reinhold

*MCA ($877.6 million) *Universal Pictures & TV; record labels; real estate developments; cemetary & park services; novelty stores.*
    Berkeley Books
    Capricorn Books
    Coward, McCann & Geoghegan
    Richard Marek Publishers
    New Times Magazine
    G.P. Putnam

MICHIGAN GENERAL ($170 million) *Concrete; paints; furniture; motor homes.*
    Pinnacle Books

**RAYTHEON CORPORATION ($2.8 billion) *Electronic systems; energy services; missiles; appliances.*
    Atheneum
    Caedmon Records
    D.C. Heath & Co.

*SCOTT & FETZER ($351.2 million) *Kirby Vacuum; air compressors; pumps; electrical products.*
    Childcraft Encyclopedia
    Science Year
    World Book Encyclopedia

*WARNER COMMUNICATIONS ($1.1 billion) *Warner Films; 6 record labels; cable communications; office buildings; cleaning services; parking lots; funeral companies.*
    D.C. Comics
    Independent News Co. (book & mag distributor)
    Mad Magazine
    Ms. Magazine (25% ownership)
    Warner Books (mass market pbk)

WESTERN PACIFIC INDUSTRIES ($212 million) *Industrial precision components; railroad.*
    Houghton Mifflin (as we go to press, Western is buying up control, with Houghton resisting)

*XEROX ($5.08 billion) *Copiers & information processing; electronics; military & aerospace technology.*
    Books in Print, other publishing directories
    R.R. Bowker Co.
    Ginn Textbooks
    Magazines (*Publishers Weekly, Library Journal, School Library Journal, Bookviews*)
    Unipub, Inc.
    University Microfilms

Booklegger, Summer 1978

PUBLISHERS ACQUIRED BY PUBLISHERS

This is a selective list due to space limits, with the largest, best known "stables" included. Among them, the poor-mouthing to authors and employees should be cut. According to *BP Report: On the Business of Book Publishing*, the top winners in book sales profits in 1977 were: Time Inc. - $46 million in pretax profits, a 17.8% profit margin; McGraw - $35.3 million, 12.6%; Scott, Foresman - $35.2 million, 19.3%; Times Mirror - $31.4 milion, 17.8%; Prentice-Hall - $31.2 million, 21.7%; Doubleday - $30 million, 9.1%. Six of the top nine mass market paperback houses boast pretax margins of 10% or better; Harlequin of Canada with a whopping 30% margin, followed by Bantam at 15-17%.

ADDISON-WESLEY ($57.1 million)
   Benjamin/Cummings Publishing Co.
   Field Educational Publishing
   Young Scott Books

BERTELSMANN (German; $120 million in sales)
   Bantam (mass market pbk; $95 million in sales)
   Peacock Press
   Transworld

CROWN ($70 million) *Joy of Sex fame; large mail order business.*
   American West Publishing Co.
   Barre Publishers
   Bonanza Reprints
   The Imprint Society
   Lenox Hill Press
   Julian Press
   Outlet Book Co. (remainders)
   Clarkson N. Potter, Inc.
   Preferred Choice Book Club
   Westover Publishing Co.

DOUBLEDAY ($300+ million) *Privately held.*
   Dell (mass market pbk)
   Dell Magazines (*Modern Screen* et al)
   Delacorte Press
   Dial Press
   Doubleday Bookstores (30)
   Doubleday Book Clubs (16, with $100 million in sales; includes the huge Literary Guild)
   Feffer & Simons, Inc.
   J.G. Ferguson Publishing Co.
   Laidlaw Brothers

DOW JONES ($317.3 million) *Financial news & services, Big Board maintenance.*
   Barron's
   Dow Books
   Richard Irwin Textbooks
   Ottaway Newspapers (13 dailies)
   Wall Street Journal

ENCYCLOPEDIA BRITANNICA *Recently ordered by FTC to cease & desist unfair sales practices.*
   F.E. Compton Company
   Library Resources, Inc.
   G. & C. Merriam

FARRAR, STRAUS & GIROUX
   Hill & Wang
   The Noonday Press
   Octagon Books

GROLIER ($221.5 million) *International; publishes largely educational and reference works. Recently ordered by FTC to cease and desist unfair sales practices.*
   Americana Encyclopedia
   Book of Knowledge
   Disney Book Club
   Marcus-Campbell Co.
   Scarecrow Press
   Franklin Watts - and many more imprints

GRUNER + JAHR AG & CO. (German)
   Parents Magazine Enterprises
   (Books, book clubs, mags, films)

*HARCOURT BRACE JOVANOVICH ($371.1 million) *Most conglomerated award. Owns fleet of 64 professional trade mags; bookstores; book clubs; exam publishers; film & media companies; as well as fish & chips chain; 3 Sea Worlds; tv stations; insurance agencies.*
   Academic Press ($49 million)
   AP Continuing Medical Education
   Beckley-Cardy Co.
   Benefic
   Grune & Stratton
   Harvest Paperbacks
   Instructor Publications
   Johnson Reprint Co.
   Jove (mass market pbk)
   Law & Business Inc.
   Media Systems College Publ.
   Voyager Paperbacks
   Weber Costello

HARPER & ROW ($114.4 million in sales)
   Abelard-Schuman
   Ballinger Publishing
   Barnes & Noble
   Basic Books, Inc.
   Canfield Press
   T.Y. Crowell
   John Day
   Dodd, Mead & Co.
   A.J. Holman
   Lippincott
   Frederick A. Stokes Co.

HEARST CORP. *Privately held newspaper & magazin chain; owns ICD, huge bk & mag wholesaler.*
   Avon (mass market pbk.; paid $1.9 million for right to *The Thorn Birds*)
   Hearst Books

*McGRAW-HILL ($659 million) *Many foreign subsidiaries. Owns fleet of professional & trade periodicals; tv stations; film & media; exam publishe data processing*
   Gregg Publishing Co.
   Herder and Herder
   Shepard's Law Citations
   Standard & Poor
   Sweet's Handbook
   Webster Publishing Co.
   Schaum Paperbacks

*MACMILLAN ($512.7 million) *Big on schools (Berlitz, LaSalle, & Katherine Gibbs, plus Ward Caps & Gowns) and stores (Brentano chain & Gump's.) Numerous book clubs & a chain of newspapers and mags. Films.*
    Benzinger, Bruce & Glencoe, Inc.
    Cleaver-Hume, Ltd.
    The Free Press
    Hafner Press
    Hagstrom Company
    P.J. Kenedy & Sons
    Schirmer Books
    Standard Rate & Data

MORGAN-GRAMPIAN (British)
    David McKay
    Charterhouse Books
    Fodor's Travel Guides
    Ives Washburn, Inc.
    Henry Z. Walck, Inc.
    Weybright & Talley, Inc.
    Peter H. Wyden

*NEW YORK TIMES ($551 million) *15 newspapers & 7 mags; TV & radio stations; timber holdings.*
    Arno Press Reprints
    Books For Libraries
    Cambridge Book Co.
    NYT Information Bank
    Quadrangle Books
    Times Books

W.W. NORTON
    Liveright Publishing Corp.

PENGUIN BOOKS (British)
    Grossman
    Viking

PRENTICE HALL ($230.6 million) *26 book clubs.*
    Appleton-Century-Crofts
    Bureau of Business Practices
    Goodyear Publishing Co.
    Institute for Business Planning
    New York Institute for Finance
    Parker Publishing Co.
    Reston Publishing Co.
    Winthrop Publishers

SCOTT, FORESMAN & CO. ($177 million)
    William Morrow & Co.
    Lothrop, Lee & Shepard Co.
    Fleming H. Revell (evangelical)
    Silver Burdett Textbooks
    South-Western Publishing Co.

SEQUOIA ELSEVIER (Dutch)
    E.P. Dutton
    Hopkins-Painter
    Phaidon Press
    Saturday Review Press

W.H. SMITH & SONS LTD. (British) *Owns 440 bookstores & 90 wholesalers in Europe.*
    Mayflower Books

LYLE STUART, INC.
    Citadel Press
    Fieldcrest Books
    Mystic Arts Book Society
    University Books, Inc.

THOMPSON EQUITABLE CORP. *Canadian international media empire.*
    Bomar Textbooks
    Noble & Noble
    Wadsworth Publishing Co.

*TIME ($1.3 billion) *4 newspapers & 5 magazines; forest product operations; investment companies; tv stations, video, & film.*
    Book of the Month Club ($65 million sales), plus numerous specialty book clubs
    Little, Brown & Company
    Lloyd Hollister, Inc.
    New York Graphic Society
    Pacifica Ltd. (Japan)
    Pioneer Publishing Co.
    Time-Life Books ($215 million; 44% sales foreign)

*TIMES MIRROR CO. ($1.1 billion) *5 newspapers; forest products; tv stations & cable.*
    Harry Abrams Art Books
    Denoyer-Geppert Co.
    Matthew Bender Law Books
    Mentor Books
    Meridan Books
    C.V. Mosby Co.
    New English Library (British pbks)
    New American Library - NAL (mass mkt pbk)
    Popular Science Publications
    Signet Paperbacks
    Southwestern Co.

*WASHINGTON POST ($426.1 million) *Newsweek; tv & radio stations; paper company.*
    Newsweek Books ($4.4 million)

JOHN WILEY & SONS, INC. ($78 million)
    Halsted Press
    Hamilton Publishing Co.
    Jacaranda Press (Australia)
    Melville Publishing Co.
    Ronald Press
    Xerox College Publications

Booklegger, Summer 1978

DULY FOOTNOTED

1"Book Publishing," by John Dessauer in *The ALA Yearbook* (American Library Association, 1976:293.) The latest Dept. of Commerce figures (1972) showed the 50 largest publishers make 77% of total sales; their universe is based on only 1,120 publishers. *Books In Print* lists 5,300 publishers; *Alternatives In Print* lists 1500 additional small publishers. The Dept. of Commerce reveals even higher concentration in the most lucrative sales categories (textbooks, technical, scientific, reference, and professional books), with 50 firms controlling 92-99% of sales. -- *Printing & Publishing*, a quarterly from Dept.of Commerce, Winter 1976:18, 25.

2"The Book Boom," *Business Week*, 7/4/77:51-2.

3"Publisher's Viewpoint: Richard E. Snyder," *Publishers Weekly*, 4/11/77:37-38.

4*Book Production Industry*, 7/76:52. Consolidation seems to have reached over-zealous proportions. 13 major paper manufacturers and 9 wholesalers indicted with conspiracy to fix prices and eliminate competition. --*PW* 9/26/77:106

5*op. cit., Business Week:*51

6*Printing & Publishing*, Winter, 1976-77:16.

7Conglomerates have a titanic obsession with Growth. See *Management by Compulsion: The Corporate Urge To Grow* by Rolf Wild, *The Conglomerate Commotion* by the Editors of Fortune, *The New Merger Game* by Dan Gussow.

8Ten chains control one-third of the daily newspaper circulation in the U.S.; 97% of the 1,544 cities in which dailies are printed are one-owner (monopoly) towns. --*U.S. News & World Report*, 8/15/77:29-30.
·Ten corporations account for 83% of all single records, albums, and tapes listed in *Billboard's* 1977 top chart action. --*Billboard*, 2/18/78:18.
·Eight companies own virtually all the top grossing films of the last 7 years, according to the 1978 *International Motion Picture Almanac*. All are conglomerated. Their strategy is to make fewer movies each year, enough to bring in a big winner or two, with most revenue coming from more predictable properties. Book publishers are attractive acquisitions because their material can be repackaged for film and tv use. --"The Cash-Rich Movie Companies: Why They Pump Box-Office Profits Into Other Businesses," *Business Week*, 5/16/77:114-24.
·Airwave ownership by network radio and tv is so entrenched most people cannot even conceive of a diversified, non-commercial public highway of communication. See Jerry Mander's *Four Arguments For The Elimination of Television*; Mankiewicz & Swerdlow: *Remote Control: TV And The Manipulation of American Life*; Eric Barnouw's *The Sponsor: Notes On A Modern Potentate*.

9Ron Busch, President of Ballantine Books: *If we had to use our own resources we'd think twice about bidding as much as we do....But with a parent or a conglomerate that has annual sales of $2 billion and up, with 2 or 3 million shareholders, what is the risk? What's the diminution of stockholder dividends if you are wrong? A mil in most cases.* --*PW*, 12/26/77:46. Dick Snyder, President of Simon & Schuster, on the $2 million auctions: *[They are] going to force an even greater consolidation of this industry. It's not even a benefit to the authors and agents either, who are basically collecting most of this money. Because so few people are involved. It's like the National Football League: the top 10 players get 99% of the money and the other 250 players get nothing.* --*PW*, 4/11/77:36.

10*The Closed Enterprise System: Ralph Nader's Study Group Report On Antitrust Enforcement* by Mark Green. (Grossman, 1972:8)

11Some money men do squawk. Author Gerard Zilg, with P.E.N. support, is suing the DuPont Co. for conspiracy to suppress Zilg's expose, *DuPont: Beyond The Nylon Curtain.* Allegedly, the DuPonts found the well-reviewed book "scurrilous," induced publisher Prentice-Hall to cease promoting it, and got BMOC to withdraw it as a selection. --*PW*, 2/6/78:24.

[12] Another Fucking Footnote: It's all happened in radio folks. When dj's on "counter-culture" fm protested commercials from ethical embarrassments like Standard Oil and Honeywell, realpolitik KSAN station manager Tom Donahue laid it out, *"Radical community stations are supported by advertisers with money. If you get in bed with the devil, you better be prepared to fuck."* FM conglomerates ABC, CBS, and Metromedia fear fucking lyrics however. Lennon's "Working Class Hero," etc. always get the bleep. For a brilliant analysis of the syndication of sound, with many parallels in publishing, see Chapple & Garofalo *Rock 'N' Roll Is Here To Pay* (Nelson-Hall, 1978.)

[13] *The New York Times* has just been sued for allegedly providing free advertising space to its subsidiary book companies, in possible antitrust violation. *PW*, 4/24/78:18.

[14] "Water, Energy, and Books - Competition Will It Help Or Hurt?" Speech by Morris Udall at AAP Convention, 1977. Reprinted in *The Congressional Record*, 6/1/77: 3432-34; a version also in *BooksWest #6*:8.

[15] "Publishing Women Form Lib Group," *PW*, 6/8/70:129.
"McGraw-Hill Picketed By Women In Publishing," *PW*, 7/6/70:35.

[16] "Let Them Eat Wood: ITT Branches Out," *New Republic*, 4/2/77:9.

[17] "Jovanovich Stuns HBJ, Industry By Firing Key Trade Dept. Employees," *BP Report*, 3/27/78:1. No notice given; guards posted to prevent fired staff from clearing out offices.

[18] "Paperback Talk," by Ray Walters. *NYTBR*, 10/23/77:51. There are 2000 varieties of shredders that eat 45% of all mass market paperbacks printed. *PW* (2/20/78:65) reports in 1977 an average of 20% of trade hardcovers were returned; 33% of mass market paperbacks. In some houses, the figures soared to 50%.

[19] *How To Get Happily Published* by Judith Appelbaum and Nancy Evans. (Harper, 1978:127.) See also "Bookworkers," *Book Magazine # 28*:5.

[20] The exception proves the rule: Katharine Graham is heir to and ruler of the *Washington Post-Newsweek*-Newsweek Books constellation. There are powerful women in the industry like Joan Manley, President of Time-Life Books, and Helen Meyer (just retired) president of Dell.
See survey of Women's National Book Assn.: "Women In Publishing: Subtle Discrimination, But Lower Pay," *PW*, 6/4/73:48.

[21] Warner Books larded the *Roots* formula with sleaze and did the *Bondmaster* trilogy "slave saga." Ads: bulging, stripped down black man pulls hot, swooning southern belle to him. This could be set to the music of Warner's record albums, advertised as "Bound To Please," picturing a bound woman with spike wheel about to tear into her crotch. Bound to happen: Warner Books pays $2½ million for paperback rights to Nixon's memoirs - sight unseen.

[22] "So Long For Now; New York's Publishing Labor Union Bids Farewell," by David Wright. *BooksWest #7*, 2/78:7.

[23] "200 Union Members Walk Out At Harper & Row," *PW*, 5/16/77:28. Sample salaries for publishing bosses: Pres. Harald Miller of Houghton Mifflin, $145,000 (1977) and Pres. Wm. Jovanovich of HBJ, $273,600 (1977).

[24] "Literary-Industrial Complex" is a phrase coined by Richard Kostelanetz, "the Grub Street Jeremiah." His excellent study, *The End of Intelligent Writing* (1974) is now available in paperback as *Literary Politics In America* (Sheed, Andrews, & McMeel, 1978.)

[25] Final foot(boot?)note: this article was rejected by nearly every one of the corporate-controlled book trade and library journals. Their survival is dependent on big publishers' ads; the independent press is accountable only to its readers.

2.

ROLL YR OWN: A Guide For New Publishers, Self-Publishers, and Authors
by Celeste West

Publishing conglomeritis may be a dread disease upon the land, but the forces of evil cannot have their way with The Word, not while The Lone Ranger of Literature still rides. Yes, The Independent Press is alive, well, and doing better than ever. Its scrappy pamphleteers, passionate poets, co-op publishing collaborateurs, letterpress artists - are all producing their own work, without benefit of The Big House.

High on new printing technology, and reaching back to the cultural revolution of the 60's, people are rolling their own: from how-to and lifestyle books that sell hundreds of thousands, to fine press editions, tailor-made textbooks and outrageous surrealia. While big publishers thrash about like fish out of water in the mass-media, independent, "alternative" publishers are finding a loyal audience and multiplying. We have rooted in the cracks and we are blossoming in the vacant lots of distribution. Establishment publishers abandoned poetry to us long ago, now fiction and social commentary are becoming ours. Every liberated front - women and third world peoples to gay libertarians and banana dadists - has its working papers: regular journals, books, broadsides and brochures. Ever since the printing press evolved from the wine press, it has been linked with renaissance and revolution. People who have something to say are simply printing it up to their own immense satisfaction.

To help, there exists a flourishing national trade association of small publishers (COSMEP). Substantial annuals like *AIP* and Dustbook's *Directory* list their output. A yearly bookfair exists in NYC to show their wares; "Women In Print" and other publishing conferences abound. Independent publishers' rallying cry is "Into Our Own Hands!" The technology is ripe; and there is excellent instruction on how to seize it. Short-run printing (50 to 5000 copies) has become a cheaper and cheaper proposition. "Instant Printing" franchises seem to multiply like MacDonald's. Anyone can print up their revelation, protest, epic poetry, or garage sale bargains for hundreds to see. You can also print hundreds of commercial-gloss, good quality copies of your work for less than the cost of a two week vacation.

If you persist in the hope a commercial New York publisher will recognize your talent, you may invest years waiting, and, for your faith get nothing but polite, withering rejections. Fact of life: most publishers do not want your work unless it has a fat, guaranteed market. Ninety percent of all manuscripts are turned down by commercial houses, according to two NY editors, Judith Applebaum and Nancy Evans. Doubleday gets 10,000 unsolicited manuscripts and proposals a year and rejects them all. They want name authors, celebs, or hot agency property. Their editors are largely fixers, who dream up a topic or repackage a formula, and get someone to do the job. Big publishers do not want brilliant avant garde writing or incendiary exposé. These don't set well with mid-west chainstore book buyers. Above all, they do not want first novels, short stories, or (Muse-have-mercy!) poetry. If you do not crank out Top Forty material, forget Tin Pan Alley. Find a small, independent publisher, or, better yet, publish it yourself.

It takes commitment though. What moves a self-publisher or a small, struggling house to go to all the bother? There is the pride of doing real work and seeing it come to fruition. There is the joy of being deeply, totally involved in producing the beauty and power of the written word. Along with these matters of the spirit, there are hard-nosed, pragmatic reasons to roll your own - even if the big boys ask you to wear their colors.

Benefits of Self-Publishing

Here are the advantages of publishing small or doing it yourself. The first is control: you say exactly what you want to say how you want to say it. Freedom of expression feels good - especially when you've had commercial editors whack your words bloodless. In addition, your book is designed the way you want it to look. You get the cover you want to live with, not an atrocity designed by someone who never even read the book. Furthermore, you get to keep all the profits if you do the job yourself, not 5 - 10% of the take. You own all subsidiary rights, not just 50% of their earnings. If you go with a small publisher, in lieu of an advance, the royalty is likely to be substantially higher than what a conglomerate publisher will pay.

You also control the promotional campaign if you do a book yourself. After all, who knows your audience best? Your book gets focused attention; it's not just one of a season's hundreds. One of the most pervasive myths regarding big house publication is that the trade-off you get for losing much control over your work is efficient, wide distribution and promotion. Poopadoodle. According to Macy's book manager, who is a vigorous book publicist herself, only around a thousand titles ever reach their full national audience. The other 35,000 or so drift. Alex Haley sued his publisher because it couldn't even get *Roots* out of the warehouse when easily predictable demand was cresting. If they can screw up a sure thing, they can really bollox the less flashy, "modest" book. Each year, New York publishers turn hundreds of new titles out on the track. The sales department never gives them equal care and handling. The sales force is told which titles are "winners." These are usually the books that cost six figures to acquire, fast-breaking "Big Books." They get the $300,000 ad budgets trumpeted to booksellers in *Publishers Weekly*. Very high sales quotas are set on such titles by the publishers. Naturally, sales reps push these assigned high-quota books, armed with big, bold ads and lots of brouhaha. Thus, the golden "bestseller" becomes its own self-fulfilling prophecy - taking the lion's share of budget and sales effort. The rest of the list is pretty much relegated to wallflower row.

No matter how loving your editor, in a big house the merchandisers are really in the saddle. If they like your work and understand your audience, great. If they are lukewarm, your book is probably going to rot in some warehouse in New Jersey. A marketing person is not your soul-mate editor; s/he may have no conception of your audience and therefore no strategy for reaching it. Example: the feminist market. A friend of mine did a brilliant book on radical women in U.S. history. Her publisher's marketing people magnanimously decided to run an ad in the *New York Times Book Review*, shining forth with a sexy testimonial by Erica Jong. Now Erica Jong is no slouch, but neither is she a prestigious historian nor heroic activist. Women interested in this book would probably be offended by such a clumsy, inappropriate tokenism. If the message was misdirected, so was this particular medium on which to blow an ad budget. The *NYTBR* readers are no way your target feminist audience. So it goes. Authors' atrocity stories about callous marketing of their books are legion. You may be lucky, but unless you know a house is totally *committed* to your book, do it yourself, or go with a small publisher. You'll sell more because there will be respect for the book and its audience. Independent, committed small publishers like Diana Press, New Glide, Daughters, etc. have sold record thousands of books which would have languished in the backwater of a big house.

In the world of commercial NY publishing, a trade book has six weeks to "make it." The shelf-life of a mass market paperback is twelve days. If it doesn't flash, it's headed for the remainder bin or shredder. A quality title with an unspectacular birth, but steady sales potential may be declared out of print just as it is finding its market. The self-publisher can keep a book alive as long as s/he wants to; in fact this is the way cult classics like Dorothy Bryant's *Kin of Ata* (née *The Comforter*) or Callenbach's *Ecotopia* have ultimately reached huge audiences. Demand momentum gradually built up, mainly by word of mouth, and the books were always there ready to move because the self-published authors believed in them.

Another advantage of self-publishing is that you can get your book out fast. It takes a large publisher twelve to eighteen months to move your manuscript through its superstructure upon acceptance. Small publishers joke, "We can have a book out in the time it takes New York to reject it." This is a function of the "Small Is Beautiful" ethos. The small and/or self-publisher is simply more adaptable, more swift, than a monolith like McGraw-Hill. Large-overhead publishers have so much riding on the success of a "property," they are likewise slow to take chances. Better at supplying a sure demand, they usually wait for the small, lithe house to create one. After the triumph of *The Whole Earth Catalog*, New York took the cue and cranked out giant-size resource books galore. In addition, big house author contracts seem carved in stone, while small houses can experiment with mutually beneficial author deals as the situation arises. Large publishers, filling orders by computer, also have notorious fulfillment snafus; in fact, the industry is almost at an impasse here. Perhaps it is all a function of media ecology: bigness breeds smallness.

Then, of course, we have the siren promise of self-publishing: "Win Love, Success, & Big Money!" This is also known as "The Trading With The Enemy Lure," but no purist am I. Let's say your women's health collective self-publishes a candid, clear (read daring) guide to women's health care. Half the population wants a copy. You go back for printing after printing. Enter Simon & Schuster. You just did their market research; you have proved this book is a winner. They beg you to let them take it on. This does actually happen - with people as diverse as the Boston Women's Health Collective, Rod McKuen, Edgar Rice Burroughs, Stewart Brand, Paula Morgan, Robert Ringer, etc. They believed they had something people wanted to read, printed up copies, demonstrated they could sell thousands, and have been courted by big publishers ever since. Moral: hot property will out (sometimes.)

Finally, there is artistic satisfaction in integrating all the processes required in creating a book. You feel every aspect flow through your veins. Once you've built a book, from the outline up, you are part of a process, rather than an isolated task force. One understands more the *entity* of the book, how the complex web of book manufacture combines the skills of printing, photography, and art. You feel the play (or sting) of silver-tongued commerce, the theater of promotion, and, if everything turns out well, how much luck and happy coincidence rule the world.

Hardships in Going It Alone

Which brings us in utter frankness, to the fact that: Everything Can Go Wrong. What's worse, if you blow it, there's no big New York house to kick around at cocktail parties. There are four major hardships in self-publishing: first of all, you risk all the money up front if you go it alone. If you join a small publisher, it can rarely put up a big advance against your projected royalties. (A small house, however, may offset this with a higher royalty percentage; thus if you win, the stakes are even sweeter.) Secondly, to birth your book, you have to absorb some printing, production, promotion, and accounting know-how. Or, you must learn enough about the trade to hire the right people to get the job done. Then, when the book is out, the time and energy requirement for sales effort takes over. Even if you hire out most of the work, books, like children and other living things, demand attention while everything else must stop.

The final hassle is coping with that old bugaboo: Stigma. Many people confuse self-publishing with "vanity," or "subsidy" publishing as it's called. Vanity publishing is a rip-off. But these "publishers" print at least two thousand titles a year and will continue to flourish as long as writers are too lazy to get out their own books or naive enough to fall for the hollow, uncritical praise dished out by such presses. An author has to pay the vanity house *all the cost of manufacture plus a fat fee.* The resulting book is a dreary standardized unit like all others the vanity press does. The books don't even belong to the author who paid for them! Vanity presses promise a high royalty on sales, but never seem to market any books. Why should they? They have back their cost plus. Booksellers, librarians, and reviewers can smell vanity publishing a mile away and won't touch it; the houses are well-known to the trade. To add injury to insult, the vanity press usually doesn't even bind more than a small percentage of copies printed. They agree to "print," not necessarily to "bind" books; binding is expensive. Their publishing contracts are models of dissimulation; send for the free reprint "Does It Pay To Pay To Have It Published?" from *Writer's Digest,* 6311 Alliance Road, Cincinnati 95242. This article cuts through all the sludge in a vanity publishing contract.

In contrast, self-publishing writers produce their own books in their own way, sub-contracting the tasks as they need to. A bit of "vanity" can certainly enter in. Writers are apt to be egocentric, ambitious, and willful. (They may also be concerned with the problem of truth, take inordinate pleasure in word magic or design aesthetics, love to store up facts for posterity, and want to change the world.) The concern of every serious writer is to get a hearing. What happens when publishers are stone deaf? They were to these self-publishers: William Blake, Thomas Paine, Nathaniel Hawthorne, Washington Irving, John Bartlett, Robert Burns, Percy Shelly, Lord Byron, Stephen Crane, George Bernard Shaw, Mary Baker Eddy, Zane Grey, Elbert Hubbard, Emily Bronte, Charlotte Bronte, Edgar Allen Poe, Horace Walpole, Lord Tennyson, Theodore Dreiser, Kate Wiggin, James Joyce, D.H. Lawrence, Ezra Pound, Henry Thoreau, Carl Sandburg, Thomas Hardy, Walt Whitman, Upton Sinclair, Mark Twain, Edgar Rice Burroughs, Virginia Woolf, Anais Nin. If you have the courage to self-publish, you are certainly travelling with quality. So much for stigma.

In the small press and self-publishing world, there is, of course, a lot of self-indulgent tripe. However, who would argue there is not a hell of a lot of shlock in commercial publishing? Actually, "subsidy publishing" is a secret little sin in which many New York commercial houses indulge. A business, institution, or government agency approaches the publisher with a proposal or manuscript they want released. They simply guarantee the publisher a certain number of sales. Such a "deal" is certainly never printed on the book, which looks like any other title. Did you ever wonder where all those *Mr. Boring Business Exec And His Rise In Corporate Good Works* came from? Not only are big egos and brand names pushed this way, but so is political propaganda. An example of "subsidy" publishing was the prestigious New York house of Praeger which in secret collusion with the USIA ground out its political "commentary" for a price. Most recently it was learned that twelve New York publishers accepted CIA slush money to publish 250 political titles. It is fair to say some houses didn't know CIA funding was behind the manuscripts they published. (See *The New York Times* series, "CIA: Secret Shaper of Public Opinion," December 25, 26, and 27, 1977.) At any rate, self-aggrandizement is clear and up front with the self-published work. Though self-publishing has some real hassles, there are ways of mitigating them. Form a co-op publishing group as advocated by Michael Cain (see his fine book, *Co-op Publishing*, listed in the resource section.) In co-op publishing, investment capital and labor are shared. As far as bare-bones publishing education: there is much information out now. The publishing "mystique" is dead. If you just read the sources listed below that are starred, you'll be pretty safe. If you are looking toward publishing as a career or want to earn economic self-sufficiency from your books, the other sources listed are very helpful.

Happily, publishing is one endeavor in which many good freelancers are available: copy editors, designers, printers, promotion people, warehousing and fulfillment services. You can act as impressario, using help where and when you need it. This requires little overhead. Large publishers have to charge up 30% to 45% of income to overhead; it probably costs them $500 to turn the lights on in the morning in a glass tower in Manhattan. But you don't need a fleet of offices, equipment or a full-time cast when you begin, or when you are between books.

Trial By Market

I would like to emphasize, however, as one who has been baptized by fire, the two areas of self-publishing fraught with danger. The first is BUDGETING. (See Resource Section III, "Finishing In The Money.") Independent, small publishers notoriously underprice their books. This is because they do not sit down and break out all the "hidden" costs. A bookstore wants 40% of your cover price; a national distributor expects at least 50%. Say your author takes 10%, and at least 20% already went to the printer. Another 10% should go for publicity and advertising. Around 5% may go for shipping costs. This leaves you only 5% to pay the rent, everyone else, and make a bit of profit - provided you sell *all* your copies. I know people who have priced their book so low, they actually *lose* money every time they make a sale. People will use every sort of whimsey in pricing their book. "A book should cost no more than $3." (Should a lunch?) "A book should cost no more than I could afford when I was a student." "A mass-market paperback costs $2.50; I have to compete." (Not unless your sales volume is 500,000 copies of junk-food for non-readers.) People will set *anything* as a price, except one arrived at by tallying costs against probable income. Recognize that you have a narrow market and a high cost per unit. It has been found books are *relatively price insensitive* - although there will be diverse purchasing power among potential buyers. Figure your real break-even, with no hidden subsidies like overhead and labor. Note: your time is a cost factor even if you don't contemplate compensation now. Quantify what you're giving away or getting free. Then, you'll know what is involved when you hire it out. Growth can be catastrophic if you are unconsciously running everything on your own subsidized labor and overhead. We blew out one magazine that way. For book cost-factors to consider, see chart inside back cover.

The second area of danger is MERCHANDISING - the hustle. Almost anyone can afford to produce a book, but not everyone can afford to market it. Small houses are usually founded by people whose primary interests are writing and editing, or perhaps design. However, the most brilliantly written, best edited, most beautiful book still has to be *sold*. To publish is to make public, and after you've created a book, half the work is still to come.

Here we introduce another rude fact of life: the imperial publishers virtually own the space in the bookstores. They have huge ad budgets to overwhelm booksellers and a fleet of sales reps who make sure their books get the space available in the stores. Display space is a scarce and valuable commodity. Bookstores calculate their turn-over in sales dollars per square foot, and woe to the book that doesn't seem guaranteed to ring the register often enough. (This is, of course, not the overriding concern in feminist, movement, and other loving bookstores, although their owners are not wild about dust-catchers either.)

Small publishers have a real chance of doing effective promotion and marketing mainly through mail order. With such direct, mail-order sales you save the 40%+ bookstore commission. Actually, most people buy their books by mail; only a thousand good, full-service bookstores exist in the country. However, there are more than one hundred and fifty book clubs, specializing in everything from gardening to gambling - and even death. (One of the latter- there are two death book clubs - is owned by a casket manufacturer. Presumably they stand to profit even when you exercise the ultimate negative option....) Millions of books are also sold to magazine coupon clippers ("SEND $9.95 TO FIND OUT HOW YOU CAN MAKE $20,000 A YEAR RAISING EARTHWORMS!!") You can buy mailing lists for almost every interest group and advertise in their media. Of course, quality fiction and poetry remain as hard for everyone to sell as yesterday's newspaper. The oasis in this bitter marketplace is Libraries. Librarians do buy some creative writing even if no one else does. Learn to market there as a vital alternative to bookstores and wholesalers. And, libraries exact no discount, nor ship back returns.

If you don't like doing the old razzle-dazzle necessary to getting your book sold, hire someone who enjoys the art of selling. This person can be a friend, who can act as agency and publicity department for a percentage of sales. Include this expense in the price of your book.

If I seem to be pushing the hors de commerce here, rather than emphasizing the soul satisfaction of publishing, it is because many creative peole will begin a publishing venture, but few can keep it going. Of course, a book's worth is not judged by its sales, but we need every grand, gifted, romantic publisher to "profit," to stay in business, to keep the doors open. Perhaps small publishing entrepreneurship is like Dr. Johnson's definition of marriage: "the triumph of hope over experience." But as long as authors matter, ideas are urgent, and words want to run like wild horses, the world needs small, independent publishers. Why will you wait, year after year?

PUBLISH-IT-YOURSELF TOOLS

I. GENERAL HOW-TO

BOOK PUBLISHING: What It Is, What It Does by John Dessauer.
1974, Bowker. 231 p. $12.50 (hdbk); $6.95 (pbk).
    The best introductory text to the haphazard, disorganized business of publishing. Dessauer, who is statistician for the Association of American Publishers and reigns as one of the industry's top consultants, explains how books are created, manufactured, and marketed by establishment publishers. You are probably not going to build your book the way the big boys do, but a lot of their techniques are worth adapting. For example, save yourself from the doom of naive pricing by studying the chapter, "How Publishers Finance, Plan, and Manage." Dessauer comes out against big publishers' take over by accountants, but he shifts into crusty conservatism with his panacea for the industry: publish less books; the distribution channels are glutted—when the point is to open more alternative communication channels.

BOOKS: From Writer To Reader by Howard Greenfield.
1976, Crown. 211p. $8.95.
    Start 'em early. This is a nice book for young adults who may have tendencies toward the worddrunk life. The author does an inspirational job in explaining all the various roles and functions involved with publishing. It's a cool, clear overview for the self-publisher too.

THE BUSINESS OF PUBLISHING: A *PW* Anthology.
1976, Bowker. 303p. $12.95.
    Typical Bowker reprint-rehash. A former Bowker employee once swore Bowker planned to do a volume called *The Way It Was*, reprints of the weather reports from the *NYT*. Here we have 42 articles from *Publishers Weekly*. Some puff, some useful info for the small publisher such as pieces on economics, manufacture, and mail order.

A CANDID CRITIQUE OF BOOK PUBLISHING by Curtis G. Benjamin.
1977, Bowker. 177p. $15.

    Benjamin is the executive who molded mighty McGraw into a member of the *Fortune 500* Club. He is a rather brusque character, who enjoys debunking cliches and conventions in publishing. Refreshing advice for the new publisher; sensible warnings about underpricing and overprinting; insider's discussions of mutinational publishing, trade associations, the paperback industry, etc. Billed as a "radical," crusty Benjamin is rather a "good liberal," who brilliantly attacks the Dessauer et al. position of "fewer and better books," but finds mergers and take-overs harmless.

CATALOGUING IN PUBLICATION: Information For Participating Publishers.
CIP Project, Library of Congress, Descriptive Cataloguing Dept., Washington, DC, 20540. 13p., free.

    Library of Congress will catalogue your book before publication so you can print all the data on your copyright page. Your book will get on the library shelf faster because each library doesn't have to repeat the cataloguing process. Bookstores also use the LC subject headings for quick shelf placement. LC prefers, but you do not have to send galleys. CAVEAT: LC is prone to *mis-* or *under*catalog women's, ethnic, prison, alternative, gay, labor, disabled, and children's books. (See *Booklegger Magazine* #15:10-12.) If you don't like LC's subject headings, demand they change them or just add your own.

THE CO-OP PUBLISHING HANDBOOK by Michael Cain.
1978, Dustbooks. 208p. $8.95 (hdbk); $3.95 (pbk).

    Co-operative publishing is synergistic self-publishing. Collaborateurs share ownership, responsibility, and product, *i.e.*, drugery & angst, power & glory. Cain examines the spirit, techniques, and motivation behind this revolutionary new mode of publishing. The co-op publishers tell their own stories (alice james books, The Fiction Collective, Lollipop Power, KNOW, Fag Rag, Berkeley Poets, etc.) Then Cain astutely analyzes their successes and failures. He brilliantly flays the imperial publishers for their pandering, but shows how the independent publisher can be a senseless egomaniac too. Buy this book: it can turn fantasy into reality; it may save your hide. One Caveat: the printer's devil at Dustbooks is a woman. Cain's mr. macho disclaimer that his sexist pronouns throughout are ok because substitutes are clumsy or "repulsive" result in his book being cursed with *a multitude* of grotesque typos.

COPYRIGHT INFORMATION:

    Write Information & Publications Section, Copyright Office, Library of Congress, Washington, D.C. 20559. Ask for their free explanatory pamphlet and some "TX" forms. All you do to register is send 2 copies of your published book, the completed and notarized TX form, and $10.

    Also check:
EXPLAINING THE NEW COPYRIGHT LAW. Association of American Publishers, 1707 L Street, N.W., DC 20036. $1.
NEW COPYRIGHT LAW PRIMER by Susan Wagner.
Order from Frieda Johnson, *Publishers Weekly*, 1180 Avenue of the Americas, NYC 10036. $1. Or, you can read it in *PW* 12/26/77:37 and 1/20/78:65.

COSMEP (Committee of Small Magazine Editors & Publishers) NEWSLETTER.
Box 703, San Francisco 94101. Monthly. $25/year membership.

    COSMEP is the publishing coalition (1150 strong!) of the independent, wild flow publishers. The *Newsletter* is a valuable forum for sharing news, support, and raging controversy. COSMEP plans to revise its technical manual on publishing later this year.

HOW TO BE YOUR OWN PUBLISHER AND GET YOUR BOOK INTO PRINT by Paul Thompson.
1978, Creative Book Co. 46p. $3.95.

    This little book is the companion volume to *Publicizing Your Self-Published Book* (see Part IV "Promotion.") Thompson describes how to get a good printing job done on your manuscript by a local printer. He wisely counsels against grand sales fantasies and large printings, but emphasizes the immense satisfaction in publishing your own words.

HOW TO GET HAPPILY PUBLISHED: A Complete And Candid Guide by Judith Appelbaum and Nancy Evans.
1978, Harper. 272p. $9.95.

    Mainly for writers who think they want into the NYC publishing thicket. Appelbaum and Evans are the frank and friendly editors (you'll rarely have), who try to ease the requisite burrs and brambles. Part I tells how to get the words written and accepted for publication. Part II is on getting the publisher to move your book, when all he really cares about is this season's blockbuster. Part III is on self-publishing; the authors make a strong, enthusiastic case for doing it yourself. Their "Resource List" (50 pages, annotated), is alone worth the price of the book. I found the schizo-sexist pronouns ingratiating, but the overall tone here is warm, sisterly, and sound.

HOW TO PUBLISH, PROMOTE, AND SELL YOUR BOOK by Joseph Goodman.
1977. Adams Press, 30 West Washington St., Chicago 60602. 65p. $3.25.

    Through four editions, this little book has calmed the fears of beginning bookmakers. It is produced by Adams Press, a short-run printer, originally for its customers. It looks like a tract (though the typeface is modernized now), and the illustrations define the word hokey. Some innaccuracies (Bowker hasn't charged for its entries for years), but *How To Publish* does offer important facts and a good grab-bag of hints, including funding and tax info. Its "Special Report On Vanity Publishing" ("tension, heartbreak, and discouragement") is high drama.

    Other short-run printers who will send you less comprehensive, but good booklets on publishing preparation are:

    CAL-SYL PRESS, 1494 MacArthur Blvd., Oakland, CA 94602. They specialize in booklets and manuals put together by educators for their classes. Their manual *How To Make A Book: A Handy Guide To Inexpensive Book Production*, 2nd ed., 80 pages is available for $2.50. Forthcoming: *How To Make A Book*, 3rd ed., 250 pages, about $9, will, according to their poet/printer, tell all.

    EDWARDS BROTHERS, 2500 South State St., Ann Arbor MI 48104. One of the largest, most successful, short-run book manufacturers. Their slick, colorful *Author's Guide To Book Planning And Production* is free.

HOW TO PUBLISH YOUR OWN BOOK: A Guide For Authors Who Wish To Publish A Book At Their Own Expense by L.W. Mueller.
1976. Harlo Press, 16721 Hamilton Avenue, Detroit 48203. 180p. $4.95.

Written by a printer who for thirty years has watched the thrills and chills of self-publishers. This should bump Goodman's *How To Publish, Promote, And Sell* as the how-to bible of the virgin publisher. It's up-to-date, lucid, and complete with a nifty section on color processing (in color.) Next to a woman, I would trust this man to print my book.

THE HUENEFELD REPORT: For Managers And Planners In Modest-Sized Book Publishing Houses.
Box U, Bedford, MA 01730. Fortnightly, $48/year.

    Written by consultants to "modest-sized" publishers (sales under $1 million/year), this service is for people who want to stay in business, minimize hassles and maximize happiness. It describes what The Imperial Publishers do and shows how to run innovative rings around them. "They're bigger, but we're faster." The 4 page *Report* focuses on one topic per issue (pricing formula, mail order tactics, electronic competition, trade terms, etc.) Besides trade information and ideas, the *Report* emphasizes methods of detailed planning, evaluation of assumptions, and precise budgeting. Back issues are available; write for list of topics.

INTO PRINT: A Practical Guide To Writing, Illustrating, & Publishing by Mary Hill and Wendell Cochran.
1977, William Kaufman. 176p. $12 (hdbk); $6.95 (pbk).

Geared toward scientists, engineers, and other professionals who want (or have) to publish, *Into Print* provides an exceptionally lucid account of the publishing process. Much of the advice is appropriate for the self-publisher, and there is a chapter devoted to this. Unique features of the book are the attention given to illustration (drawings, photos, diagrams, charts, maps, tables); indexing; show and tell (how to give interviews, graphic presentations, slide shows.) Extensive resources are listed ("Digging Deeper") for pursuing subjects further.

LITERARY MARKETPLACE 1978: With Names And Addresses.
1977, Bowker. 841p. $22.50

The contact center and supply depot of the book industry. In this fat annual you can locate book manufacturers and wholesalers, editing, graphics, permissions, promotion, and marketing people. There's a calendar of book trade events and conferences, a list of professional organizations, and more. *LMP* is available at any large library; sometimes they'll give you their old one.

ONE BOOK/FIVE WAYS: The Publishing Procedures Of Five University Presses.
Introduction by Chandler Grannis.
1977, William Kaufman. 312p. $18.95 (hdbk); $9.75 (pbk).

The American Association of University Presses commissioned this handsome procedural study in comparative publishing. University of Chicago, MIT, University of North Carolina, University of Texas, and University of Toronto Press each take the same mythical manuscript through their acquisition, editorial, design, production, and sales departments. Day-to-day routines, correspondence, and supporting documents are all shown. Because the presses' design and marketing solutions vary widely, this is a good book for a publishing course. The financial projection sheets and contracts are useful studies for the small publisher.

THE PUBLISH-IT-YOURSELF HANDBOOK: Without Commercial Or Vanity Publishers edited by Bill Henderson.
1973, Pushcart Press. 363p. $11.95 (hdbk); $5 (pbk).

Mainly *why* to publish your own, rather than basic how-to. Dauntless spirits from Anais Nin and Leonard Woolf to Barbara Garson and Stewart Brand celebrate the great literary tradition of going it alone. *The Handbook* has a rags to riches story of its own: now in its 8th printing, the book became a sensation partially because its publishers were good at massaging the establishment media. They now do "best of the small press" anthologies, selling the rights to a mass market paperback house.

PUBLISHERS WEEKLY: The Book Industry Journal.
Box 67, Whitinsville MA 01588. Weekly, $30/year.

The trade magazine of publishers and booksellers. Lots of news, tricks of the trade, razzle-dazzle reviews. If you like show biz, you'll love *Publishers Weekly*.

A WRITER'S GUIDE TO BOOK PUBLISHING by Richard Balkin.
1977, Hawthorn. 236p. $9.95. *Appendices:* "Sample Book Proposal," "A Sample Reader's Report," "A Sample Contract."

There is a huge amount of material on how to get published. More people seem to make money off of writers than off readers. However, Balkin's book is a real find for the aspiring writer as well as the new publisher. A former editor, now literary agent, Balkin provides a good summary of the publishing process. The writer who understands the scene can be optimally involved all along the way. This is important as more commercial publishers' energy is being diverted by the Blockbuster Book. Balkin also includes a long chapter on the alternative press and self-publishing as a viable route.

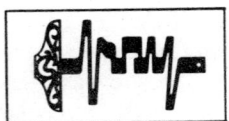

II. DESIGN, GRAPHIC TECHNIQUES, & PRINTING

The visual design of a book is as important to the work as it is to a play or building. Every book has graphic and tactile characteristics which can be organized to the advantage of the author and the reader. Go to a bookstore or library and see what it is that makes some books give you an irrepressible desire to page them. Thanks to the wonders of modern technology and a few design tricks, you can be economical and still create such an attraction. If you can't do your own design and production, there are numerous freelancers you can hire. Most of your budget goes to production; you might as well have it done right. Read the sources below to understand the argot, find ideas, and not get in over your head.

BOOK PRODUCTION INDUSTRY & MAGAZINE PRODUCTION.
Box 429, Saugatuck Station, Westport CT 06880. Bimonthly, $10/year; or free to you "in the trade": request on letterhead as "production manager."

Flamboyantly bound with paper stocks galore, *BPI* waves the wares of the printing, binding, paper, and composition industries. It is designed for high roller production managers, but even if you don't know Tyvek spunbound olefin from cambrics and hollands, *BPI* packs much information on the technology you are buying. Each September issue is a directory of paper and binding suppliers and book manufacturers. *BPI* also covers publishing news (finances, trends, mergers, conferences.) There are well written articles, both technical ("Factors Affecting Book Opening") and wide-ranging ("The Woman Behind The Books At Time, Inc.") Ads go from sensible to sexist: see Union Oil Co. jack-off every issue with its hot melt adhesive....

BOOKMAKING: The Illustrated Guide To Design by Marshall Lee.
1965, Bowker. 399p. $18.95.

There are many useful "commercial art" type books oriented toward magazine and advertising copy preparation. There are works at the other end of the spectrum concerned with Book As Art: the fine press esthetic. Lee's book is a nice meld of both worlds, itself an elegant statement of graphic and tactile beauty. Lee has a Taoist sense of book building: harmonious, creative, practical. His book fully outlines the procedures of ordinary bookmaking (castoff, composition, lay-out, design); includes reams of information (offset presswork, cost estimating, paper, binding); and is profusely illustrated.

THE DESIGN OF BOOKS by Adrian Wilson.
1974, Peregrine Smith. 160p. $6.95.

A handsome, meaningful book by a master designer. Wilson touches on the history and tradition of book design, shows exactly how the book designer prepares lay-outs, and discusses type, printing processes, paper and binding. *Design* is filled with samples of award winning works which break all the rules of conformist design, while being marvellously appropriate. "The Designer's Questionnaire" (page 69) is a good checklist for self-publishers to use in planning an integrated book.

EDITING BY DESIGN: Word-And-Picture Communication For Editors and Designers by Jan V. White.
1974, Bowker. 230p. $17.95.

Actually focuses on magazine design, but exuberates the *joi de vivre* in learning a visual vocabulary. White whips up good (not always lavish) recipes for expressive communication. Many of the ingredients: space, style, typography, color, photos, drawings, and graphic tools have application in book presentation. Best of all, his recipes tell why something works - or flops.

FINE PRINT: A Review For The Arts Of The Book.
Box 7741, San Francisco 94120. Quarterly. $12/year individuals; $14/year institutions.

If you want to get into the world of finely printed books, calligraphy, design, papermaking, and bookbinding, this handsome magazine is a showcase of the bibliophile's art.

See also the special supplement to *The San Francisco Review of Books* (December 1977) called "The Book Arts: Contemporary Fine Printing In The Bay Area," a fascinating look at the letterpress capital of the nation, with good guides for the beginner.

FROM COVER TO COVER: The Occasional Papers Of A Book Designer by Stefan Salter.
1969, Prentice-Hall. 270p. $9.95.

Charming, chatty meanderings on the life and times of an eminent book designer/lover. There isn't a lot of step-by-step technique (except a real life drama in the meticulous math of manuscript castoff.) But the book is good grounding for one concerned with freelancing, maintaining personal principles in a sometimes crass industry, and with building a "philosophy" of design.

HOW TO DO LEAFLETS, NEWSLETTERS, AND NEWSPAPERS by Nancy Brigham.
1976. New England Free Press, 60 Union Sq., Somerville MA 02143. 8½ x 11", 44p. $1.55.

HOW TO PUBLISH INFORMATION ON AN INCREDIBLY TIGHT BUDGET by Vic Pawlak. 1977. Do It Now Foundation, Box 5115, Phoenix AZ 85010. 22p., $.50.

BASICS. From paste-up to print-out, these booklets get the bon marché-bargain award for delivering the clearest light for the least money and nonsense. They are written for activists who want to publish political information, but don't have graphic arts know-how. Good practical reading, writing, and revolution.

AN INTRODUCTION TO DESIGN POETICS: A Primer With Manifesto by Denis Boyles.
1975. Assembling Press, Box 1967, NYC 11202. 62p. $3.

Now that you've learned all the conventions of print design, don't be hidebound. Literary artiste Boyles rubber-stamped a train voyage story on a 30 yard piece of muslin. The muslin moves while the reader sits in a chair as the story passes by. "Just like a train." Or - beat the shredder with squares of plexiglass, dress shop mannequins, styrofoam cubebooks. Remember folks, only the self-publisher can construct a three-dimensional adjective. (See page 48 for a catalog of artists' books.)

LITHOGRAPHER 3 & 2 by The Bureau Of Naval Personnel.
1975. (Stock 008-047-00190-3.) Order from Superintendent of Documents, GPO, Washington, DC 20402. 557p. $6.05.

Most print shops have a copy of this "bible." An exhaustive reference manual, it covers everything from preparing copy to repairing presses. Superb diagrams and illustrations. There are conventional textbooks for printers, but this manual is cheap and complete.

OFFSET - GRAPHICS, PRINTING, BINDING by Western World Press, Box 2714, Culver City CA 90230. 1977. 48p. $1.

Offbeat little guide to the world of offset printing equipment and composing machines. An "improvisation" on a full blown manual to arrive later this year, it is now editorial and design mayhem. But the technical advice is valuable. The booklet is especially worthwhile if you are considering investing in equipment or just want to understand how offset works so you can prepare good copy for the printer.

POCKET PAL: A Graphic Arts Digest For Printers & Advertising Production Managers. 1978. International Paper Co., Box 100, Church Street Sta., NYC 10046. 192p. $2.50.

A nifty book you also find in a a lot of print shops. This concise, colorful handbook, now in its 11th edition, is packed with facts on printing processes and equipment, art and copy preparation, paper, inks. Such good public relations for International Paper Co., see next entry for the competition....

"THE PRIDE PROGRAM: Programs Relating To Industry Developments & Education." Majestic Paper Corporation, 161 Hudson St., NYC 10013.

If You Are Ever In New York Department: Majestic Paper has a library of 50+ hours of video tapes on technical aspects of the graphic arts. There are programs by the industry's leading experts on typography, paper, photography, printing, inks, chemicals, binding. They are free; all you have to do is get there and set up a time in their viewing room. This is complete with a gleaming, miniaturized paper making machine that pulps wood chips at one end, then bleaches, beats, compresses and squeeze dries them into paper at the other.

PRINTING FOR THE MOVEMENT by The Great Atlantic Radio Conspiracy.
1974. GARC, 2743 Maryland Ave., Baltimore 21218. ½ hour audio-cassette, $3.50.

A little non-linear relief here. This cheery tape interviews experts who tell all about printing up the revolution on offset - or mimeo and electric stencil. You hear how presses and typesetting work, about layout and paste up, when and how to buy equipment - all set to the up-tempo of mighty presses clacketing and good ole 60's rock.

PRINTING IT: A Guide To Graphic Techniques For The Impecunious by Clifford Burke. 1972, Wingbow Press. 127p., $3.

How to be graphically beautiful, fascinating, or at least appropriate on little money. You need skills, information, practice, well-selected tools and materials, and *care*. Burke, fine press printer and designer, points the way for the novice publisher of flyers, posters, and books.

PRINTING TYPES: An Introduction by Alexander Lawson.
1971, Beacon. 120p. $2.95.

Once intoxicated with typography, you can devote your life to study of The Black Art. Many people do. There are whole encyclopedias on the subject. This handsome little book is an introduction to the typeface "families." It touches on the history and development of faces, but really focuses on recognition and classification, so you can find your way around in this subtle and sophisticated art.

TYPEWORLD: The Newspaper For The Word Processing and Typographic Community.
15 Oakridge Circle, North Wilmington, MA 01887. Monthly, free.

Take a walk on the wild side - of electrostatic communication. Here is the ultimate in present and future typesetting technology. This 32 page tabloid reports the latest hardware components: phototypesetting processors; video computers; transmitters (there's a laser in your future); scanners; cathode monitors; soft plotters; on-line interfaces....gosh. Also information on new typefaces; conferences on the print and graphic arts; well-written pieces on the industry. Again, you may not know a "baud" from a "buffer" or ever expect close encounters with a "volatile display" in your "duplex," but this little paper is guaranteed to keep out the "type lice."

WOMEN AS PRINTERS by Lois Rather.
1970 Limited Edition (150 copies.) Rather Press, Oakland, CA. 73p., out of print.

This fine hand-set book, produced with love and erudition, makes you feel like you did when you were young and opened a book and time stopped. Treasure island. If you love printing and you love women, when you come to San Francisco (you will), read it at San Francisco Public Library, Special Collections. Researchers watch out: if you follow the foot-notes, you'll be on the trail the rest of the year. Favorite fantasy generated: women once more become the official government printers and refuse to set stupid laws. (Six women in colonial times were designated government printers; one, Dinah Nuthead, was illiterate (!) and signed by mark. A woman, Mary Katherine Goddard, printed the official copy of the Declaration of Independence.) Here is the first feminist act in the Gutenberg Galaxy: An anonymous (natch) woman in fifteenth century Germany got into a printshop when it was deserted and "corrected" the type set up for printing so as to alter the verse *Genesis III:16:*

> *Unto the woman He said, I will greatly multiply thy sorrow and thy conception; in sorrow thou shalt bring forth children; and thy desire shall be to thy husband, and he shall rule over thee.*

Instead of the traditional ending, she substituted the words, *"and he shall be thy fool."* It is said that "her life paid for the alteration" undiscovered until some copies had been distributed.

Read on to find out how, despite repressive guilds and unions, as well as cultish male bibliographic societies, Women Ran Presses!

On the history of women in printing see also "WOMEN: A Special Issue," of *Journalism History* (I:4 Winter 1974-75.) Available from Journalism Dept., Darby Annex 103, Cal State, Northridge, CA 91324. 47p. $2.25

III. FINISHING IN THE MONEY

Publishing is a high risk business: the true sport of queens. It is completely alien territory for the classic grad-grind "economic man" mandated to "maximize profits and minimize losses." What one has to learn in publishing is, between winners, how to sustain losses - preferably in style. Establishment publishers play their subsidiary rights, backlists, and bank loans when outside that circle of roses. The small publisher needs a scam too (a long-distance-runner title, personal savings, rich lovers, free-lance skills), but does not have the same crushing overhead to shore-up. S/he can perhaps just let things lie fallow until the old fever rises again. However, it is no fun to play if one comes limping home each time out.

Moral: get business-wise. True, no tool of economic analysis can replace your splendid intuition, taste, or judgment. Nor can any skilled accounting technique eliminate risk. However, knowing the basic break-even economics of publishing is as important as being able to read the tote board at the tracks. If you can't calculate your cash flow and realistically budget your operations you will lose your investment stillborn. You've got to know simple cost-accounting or hire someone who does. Accounting is like housework; it's never done and never fun. But, without it, you'll get in hopeless, depressing tangles.

If publishing is not your career, but a fine diversion or passionate sideline, be crystal clear about your costs anyway. It's more fun to break all the rules when you know that you are. Budget a calculated loss just as carefully as you budget a calculated gain. When you understand the dynamics of having your cake and eating it too, you can prolong the banquet....

"THE ECONOMICS OF SCHOLARLY PUBLISHING," Chapter 5 in *To Advance Knowledge: A Handbook On American University Press Publishing* by Gene R. Hawes. 1967, American University Press Services.

Crystal clear discussion of any short-run book's break-even economics. Beginning with George Brockway's classic model illustrating why most trade books lose money, the article details each operation you must complete (manufacturing, promotion, order processing, etc.) as an item of cost and summarizes it in a break-even calculation. If you don't now understand terms like "overhead," "plant costs," "inventory write-down," you will.

"FLOWS, SEQUENCES, & DECISIONS," (Chapter 3) and "THE ECONOMICS OF MICROPUBLISHING," (Chapter 4) in *The Art & Science of Book Publishing* by Herbert S. Bailey.
1970, Harper.

One way to become successful in business is to *seem* successful. One way to seem successful is to talk like you went to the Harvard Business School of Publishing. Bailey, though of Princeton University Press fame, has got the rhetoric to copy when you go to borrow money. Make color-coded models of his labyrinthe flow charts, flexous graphs, and intricate formulae to put up on your bulletin board; your family and friends will think you know what the hell you're doing.

THE HUENEFELD GUIDE TO BOOK PUBLISHING by John Huenefeld.
1978, The Huenefeld Corp., 119 Great Road, Bedford, MA 01730.
$88; Forthcoming July 1978.

This guide is a revision to *How To Make Money Publishing Books* (1974) and to *Vinebrook Documents: Business Forms For A Small Book Publisher* (1974). These loose-leaf manuals were motherlodes of publishing management and business techniques, of examples and forms. Expensive, but if you are into publishing more than a one-shot book you totally subsidize, *The Guide* can save you years of experience, hours of planning, and prevent expensive oversights.

"HOW I SUCCEEDED AS A SMALL PUBLISHER BY BREAKING ALL THE RULES" by John Stevens.
Publishers Weekly, 10/18/76:32-34.

True life zen-simple adventures of the innovative founder of Real People Press. His methods: *precisely* thought-out goals and guidelines; few, but quality titles; no space advertising; stripped-down business procedures; low overhead; stay small.

"THE MONEY SIDE OF PUBLISHING: Fundamentals For Non-Financial People."
(Report of a 1976 conference sponsored by the Assn. of American Publishers.) Order from AAP, One Park Avenue, NYC 10016. 41p., $3.

Proceedings from a conference held to raise the cost consciousness of editors at The Big House. If you don't think "discounted cash flow," "return on investment," "amortization by the sum of the digits method," or "throughput matrix" are witty and charming topics, you don't know New Yawk publishers. I would take some of the patter with a twist of lemon, but there is enough solid bottom-line stuff here to be useful.

POSTAL SERVICE MANUAL, Chapter I (Post Office Services - Domestic).

Just cruise this at a large library. Get *"New Domestic Postage Rates,"* an 11 page bulletin, free from your local P.O. Unless you pay a distributor 50%+ of your cover price in order to escape the haggles of billing and the hassles of shipping, You Must Do Battle With The U.S. Postal Service And Survive. If you don't master its rules & canons, you will lose money, labor, shipments, and whole promotional campaigns. Of course, since the Nixonian "Reorganization Act," you will anyway. Book rate is going up substantially in 1979. Hottest tips: know the 64% lower rates for shipping to schools and libraries; the "Special Handling" speed-up; insure *everything* you can't afford to lose.

PUBLISHERS WEEKLY: The Year In Review. (1977 Book Trade Statistics - 2/20/78:65.)

Each February, as well as in summer, *PW* reports on commercial publishers' net dollar sales, volume sold, title output, average price by books' subject category, etc. Interesting to see where you fit in the Big Book Universe. (Independent presses go largely unreported here.) Items: sales are up to $4.6 billion now, increasing because of higher prices, not unit sales. Average 1977 hdbk price was $18.03; trade pbk $5.89; mass market $1.71. Most books are sold by mail. All these statistics are summarized at the end of the year in *The Bowker Annual*.

PUBLISHING: The Creative Business by Harold Bohne and Harry Van Ierssel.
1973, University Of Toronto Press for The Ontario Arts Council. 92p. $5.25.

Although a few pages deal specifically with Canadian rights, and it does not address distribution methods, this guide is fundamental to an understanding of the industry's unique accounting procedures and business operations. A clear text with sample forms, agreements, budgets, and financial statements make this a fine manual for the new publisher who prefers a five-year plan to improvising and juggling cash flow.

"PRICES, PRINTINGS & PROFITS: How To Draw The Bottom Line" by Thomas McCormack.
Publishers Weekly, 8/15/77:34-41.

The president of St. Martin's Press looks at factors affecting profitability and explains how to calculate your odds and evaluate your performance. Heavy going, but in the ocean of accounting exotica, you can distill some useful concepts. It's also fun to read how the big trade publishers have been using the wrong accounting formulae for years. This is one reason the industry's average cost of sales is 62.8% and its average overhead is 50.7%; i.e., if it weren't for subsidiary rights, they would lose 13.5% on their investment each year!

 SMALL-TIME OPERATOR: How To Start Your Own Business, Keep Your Books, Pay Your Taxes, And Stay Out Of Trouble! by Bernard Kamoroff.
1976. Bell Springs Publishing Co., Box 322, Laytonville, CA 95454. 190p. (includes ledgers & worksheets.) $6.95.

This manual is not about publishing enterprises, *per se*. Get it if you know something about publishing, but nothing, absolutely nothing, about business. Kamoroff, a hip CPA, provides the basic record-keeping and legal information you need to set up shop. He was also enterprising enough to publish this book himself and make big bucks.

IV. PROMOTION

Lots of people may want your book, but won't have the faintest idea it exists. You probably can't afford space advertising ($5,500 a page in the *NYTBR*; $1080 a page in *Library Journal*), but if you can get listed and get reviewed, the world will came to your door - if not in droves, at least in reassuring numbers. The four books listed below reveal all the pitch techniques: promotion, publicity, and advertising. Our "Review Media" list (p. 34) consists of bare basics, so at the library check *Ulrich's International Periodical Directory* too. It is arranged by subject area (astrology, dance, music, printing, women, etc., even "adventure and romance.") You can find there which magazines relate to your book's specific interest. They may run a review, news item, or feature on it. They may even buy serial rights to a chapter. Be persistent, polite, and pushy.

If you don't make an effort to reach the "Media" on page 34, you are hiding your book under a bushel. (Image of desolation row, stillborn infant, hanging fire....) Also check *Literary Market Place* for contacts. We list important independent press, feminist, and library free press in the next chapters. See why you have to budget for at least one hundred review copies?

May the great god Biblios bless you and your rave notices.

AMERICAN ODYSSEY: A Book Selling Travelogue by Len Fulton and Ellen Ferber.
1975, Dustbooks. 184p. $4.50.

　　The owners of the legendary Dustbooks, fastest draw in the West, burnt 10,000 miles of track across the nation to peddle their books in 275 bookstores in 42 days. "We sold books in bookstores , sometimes one at a time, and sometimes none. It was a process to drive market researchers mad. We also gave them away, bartered and traded with them... And we saw America, in parking lots and toilets, in malls and dry washes, on highways, in cities, on ridges, through trees....Selling has no middle ground that I can see. It has no point of rest. Its root in the medulla oblongata is tension and vulnerability - you are always vulnerable whether you are selling or being sold." Winners of the True Grit Award for uncrass commercialism.

HOW TO SELF-PUBLISH YOUR OWN BOOK AND MAKE IT A BEST SELLER: by Ted Nicholas.
1975, Enterprise Publishing Co. 167p. $14.95.

　　You're a sensitive artiste who has just published your masterpiece. You read this book; you throw up. Nicholas is a millionaire, the prototype jive-talking, snake-oil supersales bozo who did the sloppy job on *How To Form Your Own Corporation Without A Lawyer For Under $50.00*, and parlayed its sales into hundreds of thousands. Gawd, the man can hustle. And, basically, his "crass" advice is good: you have to become your own public relations consultant and your own ad agency -- or your book is dead. So use Nicholas' "game plan," polish up his sample come-ons, build that mailing list. Even if you don't "pyramid your profits" into greater ad campaigns and further glory, at least you'll move some stock.

PUBLICIZING YOUR SELF-PUBLISHED BOOK, Or, How To Do It Yourself If The Big Outfit Won't by Herman Blackey.
1976, Creative Book Co. 48p. $3.95.

　　Another simple format, 8½ x 11" typewritten, how-to from the folks who brought you *How To Be Your Own Publisher*. This one tells you how to beat the drums: news releases, press kits, mailing lists, parties, radio & tv, agents, ads, flyers, catalogs, the lecture circuit. Includes lots of examples from the establishment and the independent press. You may not be up for a promotion party after the local church service, but this book has a lot of good ideas even the shy author could bring off.

THE WRITER PUBLISHER, *Appendix* "A Book's Calendar" by Charles Aronson.
1976. Charles Aronson, RRI, Hundred Acres, Arcade NY 14009. 30p. $1.

　　Aronson wrote *Writer Publisher* (384p., $4.95) about tangling with a shoddy vanity press and then becoming a publisher himself to get the job done right. The book is a little purple, but its appendices, "A Book's Calendar," available separately, provide a crucial checklist of things to do to make sure your book is listed in the national bibliography and is well publicized.

CHECKLIST OF MEDIA AND ANNUAL DIRECTORIES TO GET IN

"ABOUT BOOKS."
American Library Association, 50 East Huron, Chicago 60611. *Syndicated column which appears in many newspapers.*

ALTERNATIVES IN PRINT.
New Glide, 330 Ellis St., San Francisco 94102. *Directory.*

AMERICAN BOOK NEWS.
Box 7458, Dallas 75209.

AMERICAN BOOK REVIEW.
Box 188, Cooper Union Station, NYC 10003. *New monthly, fair-haired child of NEA.*

AMERICAN LIBRARIES MAGAZINE.
50 East Huron, Chicago 60611. *Circulation: 37,000.*

BOOKLIST.
50 East Huron, Chicago 60611. *Send a copy to the general reviews editor and one to Val Morehouse, Box 1172, Plymouth , MA 02360, who does a small press column. Circulation 38,000.*

BOOKSWEST.
3757 Wilshire Blvd., LA 90010

BOOKS IN PRINT.
1180 Avenue of the Americas, NYC 10036. *Directory.*

CHOICE.
100 Riverview Drive, Middletown, CT 06457. *Goes to 6000 college librarians.*

CUMULATIVE BOOK INDEX
950 University Ave., Bronx, NY 10452. *Directory.*

FORECAST.
1515 Broadway, NYC 10036. *Published by Baker & Taylor, usa's largest & most mixed-up book wholesaler. If they take on your book, look forward to increased sales and greater fulfillment snafus.*

HORN BOOK MAGAZINE.
585 Boylston St., Boston 02166. *Kids books. Circulation 25,000.*

INTERNATIONAL DIRECTORY OF LITTLE MAGAZINES & SMALL PRESSES.
Box 100, Paradise, CA 95969. *Directory.*

LIBRARY JOURNAL.
1180 Avenue of the Americas, NYC 10036.*Send a copy to the general reviews editor and one to Bill Katz, School of Library Science, SUNY, 1400 Washington Avenue, Albany, NY 12203. Katz & Co. cover the small press scene for LJ.*

KIRKUS REVIEWS.
60 W. 13th St., NYC 10011. *You have to send pre-publication galleys. Reviews tend to be rather third-cocktail, witty and inchoate.*

LOCAL NEWSPAPER, RADIO, AND TV.
Your book is news - fascinating, informative, local color. Small publishers are often rewarded in their own country.

NEW YORK REVIEW OF BOOKS.
250 W. 57th St., NYC 10019. *Owns Kirkus (above.) Clubby. Circulation 89,000.*

NEW YORK TIMES BOOK REVIEW.
Times Square, NYC 10036. *Circulation 1½ million; readership 4 million. Sometimes they leave the backdoor unlocked....*

PUBLISHERS WEEKLY.
1180 Avenue of the Americas, NYC 10036.*Circulation 33,000. Their early warning system also requires pre-publication galleys.*

THE REAL PAPER.
929 Massachusetts Ave., Cambridge, MA 02139.

SAN FRANCISCO REVIEW OF BOOKS.
2140 Vallejo, SF 94123.

SATURDAY REVIEW.
1290 Avenue of the Americas, NYC 10019.

SCHOOL LIBRARY JOURNAL.
1180 Avenue of the Americas, NYC 10036. *Kids and young adult books. Circulation: 41,000.*

SELECT PRESS REVIEW.
14 South St., Milford, NH 03055. *Published by Select Press Book Service, a distributor who may take on your book.*

SMALL PRESS REVIEW.
Box 1056, Paradise, CA 95969.

SOHO WEEKLY NEWS.
111 Spring St., NYC 10012.

VILLAGE VOICE.
80 University Place, NYC 10003.

WASHINGTON POST BOOK WORLD.
1150 15th St., NW, Washington, DC 20071.

WEST COAST REVIEW OF BOOKS.
6311 Yucca St., Hollywood, CA 90028.

WESTERN PUBLISHING SCENE.
Box 1275, San Luis Obispo, CA 93406. *News releases only.*

WILSON LIBRARY BULLETIN.
950 University Ave., Bronx, NY 10452. *Circulation 26,000.*

V. EDUCATION FOR PUBLISHING

"By any measure, America's publishing education is, in comparison with Germany, England, Japan, and France, that of an underdeveloped country," declares a report issued last year by the Education For Publishing Committee of the Association of American Publishers. Again quoting the 103 page report, aptly titled *The Accidental Profession:* "The accidental nature of publishing contributes to its spontaneity, liveliness, charm, rewards, and broken fortunes...."

Publishing is a trade traditionally learned by the apprenticeship method, with requisite low pay for neophytes. But the *glamour!* the *up*town status! Eager literary types from the Seven Sisters (and Low Rent smart kids) become typists and readers in the publishing houses, and, hopefully, work their way up to become editors. Men simply become editors - or hustle in as sales reps, thereby learning publishing economics on the road. The people who learn the money-end get the power. The people who stick with culture get long lunches.

The best way to be part of this syndrome is to go to NYC and indenture yourself to a house. Attending one of the courses listed below can help you get a foot in the door; you may meet someone important who casts a kind eye on you. If you prefer the unkept life - setting up your own show, fraught with risk, unknown horrors, "broken fortunes," and less prestige - it's still a good idea to get experience for awhile with someone else paying the overhead. These courses are ill-designed for the entrepreneur, but you can learn some tricks. Radcliffe is the oldest and most traditional ("Ladies, brush up on those typing skills!") NYU is quite intensive, with good field trips. Stanford is featuring a special seminar on "stress management" this year. There are also regular institutes given in large cities by professional consultants such as the Center For Direct Marketing, Huenefeld Corporation, Knowledge Industries, and Bowker. They are listed in *PW*. See also the "Courses For The Book Trade" section of *Literary Market Place*. The Association of American Publishers now has funding to begin in July an "Education For Publishing" program. It will have a full-time director to develop model courses for colleges.

ANNUAL COURSES & INSTITUTES IN PUBLISHING

BOOK MANUFACTURERS' INSTITUTE. "Yearly Seminar For Book Publishing Production Personnel." Presented in cooperation with Rochester Institute of Technology (see below.) Contact Douglas Horner, BMI, 111 Prospect St., Stamford, CT 06901. *Geared to production people who do not have a formal background in composition, printing, and binding technology. One week, Spring.*

UNIVERSITY OF DENVER. "Publishing Institute." School of Librarianship, Denver 80208. Elizabeth Geiser, Director. *Four weeks, Summer. $625.*

LIBRARY SCHOOLS. *Besides Denver, Emory University, SUNY, and Simmons, about ten other library schools have been known to offer occasional classes in publishing.*

LOCAL UNIVERSITY EXTENSION COURSES. *Many schools that have writing classes will have special publishing institutes. UC does this about twice a year; so does Hunter. You can request extension or your city college, or free university to invite a local publisher to present a course.*

NEW YORK UNIVERSITY. "Book Publishing In New York." School of Continuing Education, 2 University Place - Room 21, NYC 10003. Raymond Zelazny, Director. *Four weeks; Summer. $750.*

RADCLIFFE UNIVERSITY. "Publishing Course." 10 Garden St., Cambridge, MA 02138. Diggory Venn, Director. *Six weeks, Summer. $850.*

ROCHESTER INSTITUTE OF TECHNOLOGY. School of Printing, Rochester, NY 14623. *The prestigious School of Printing, now moving toward 10% women, is the place to go if you want a career in production or graphic arts. Degree programs and special institutes are offered.*

SARAH LAWRENCE COLLEGE. "Publishing Laboratory." Office of Summer Programs, Bronxville, NY 10708. *Four weeks, Summer. $675.*

STANFORD. "Publishing Course." Write Della van Heyst, Director of Publications, Stanford Alumni Assn., Bowman Alumni House, Stanford, CA 94305. *Two weeks, Summer. $425.*

3.

DISCOVERING THE WILD & FREE PRESS:
Where The Independents Do It & Deal It

by Valerie Wheat

The title of this chapter is action-oriented because independent publishers still have to be virtually "discovered." With their frequent address changes, financial fluctuations and invisibility in review media and bookstores, independent presses offer a real challenge to the prospective buyer or aficionado. These publishers can't afford huge advertising campaigns, seldom publish big names or get their authors on television talk shows. As illustrated in "The Literary/Industrial Complex," publishing literally *is* big business. Small press people have not been businesslike enough in terms of their volunteer labors of love, underpriced books and haphazard publicity.

But there is a new spirit of coordination and an awareness of the problems librarians and others face in keeping up with the proliferation of publishers. The following "Access Tools" will help to locate and elaborate on independent publishers. "Alternative Review and News Media" listed in the second section offer a consistent record of new publications, authors and organizations. There is almost no duplication of titles reviewed by these alternative media and those reviewed by *Library Journal, Publishers Weekly* and other establishment journals. The "Selected Distributors" in section three help alleviate the problem of where to buy what you read about and offer some centralization to institutional buyers. Of course, not every publication coming from these presses is good nor every one from the biggies bad. But it does seem that a greater proportion of these books and magazines have a reason to exist, a spark of life not artificially inseminated by computer formula or in response to a hot sales phenomenon. Use this guide to chart your own explorations into diverse and untamed territory.

I. GUIDES, DIRECTORIES, INDEXES

ALTERNATIVE PRESS INDEX.
Alternative Press Centre, Box 7229, Baltimore 21218. Quarterly. Just out is Volume 7, Number 4 indexing Oct./Dec. 1975. 111p. Subscriptions for Volume 7 (1975) $15/indiv.; $25/high schools and movement groups; $60/library and educational instit.; $75/military and corporate instit. Back issues available and a free list of 225 alternative press publications.

This "Radical Reader's Guide" subject indexes about 160 alternative newspapers and magazines, including book and film reviews (though not every issue of every publication is represented). The collective is on a firm footing now, quickly catching up on the backlog, and its efforts deserve support. Many of these periodicals are indexed *nowhere* else (not *Access*, *Popular Periodical Index* or the *New Periodicals Index*).

ALTERNATIVES: A Guide to the Newspapers, Magazines, and Newsletters in the Alternative Press Collection in the Special Collections Department of the University of Connecticut Library by Joanne Akeroyd.
2nd ed. 1976. From Acquisitions Dept., University of Connecticut Library, Storrs, CT 06268. 128p. $3 prepaid.

Lists 1500 periodicals by title with place of publication (but not complete address) and dates of their holdings. Also indexed under 200 subject headings and by geographic area. The present (labor, youth liberation) and past (GI movement and head comix) viewed through prisms of *Just Economics*, *Wassaja*, *Daily Planet*, even the *Buddhist Third Class Junk Mail Oracle!*

ALTERNATIVES IN PRINT: Catalog of Social Change Publications.
5th ed. 1977. Compiled by the SRRT Task Force on AIP. From New Glide Publications, 330 Ellis St., San Francisco 94102. 198p. $12.95 (hdbk); $8.95 (pbk) + $.50 postage.

In a new 8½x11" format, the latest *AIP* bursts with over 25,000 titles from 1500 alternative organizations and presses (the first edition in 1973 included only 200). All publishers are listed by subject and then in alphabetical order. Entry includes titles and order information for all their books, tapes, records, pamphlets, films, posters or comics. A glorious diversity: poetry, polemic and the path with heart. An additional listing by state of all publishers and groups with addresses makes a handy mailing list.

BOOK PUBLISHERS DIRECTORY: An Information Service Covering New and Established, Private and Special Interest, Avant-Garde and Alternative, Organization and Association, Government and Institution Presses. Edited by Elizabeth Geiser and Annie Brewer.
Gale Research Company, Book Tower, Detroit 48226. Quarterly, Number 1 June 1977. Subscription $75/year.

First issue has 695 entries listing address and telephone, date founded, officers names, number of titles per year, discount and returns policy, and a brief description with sample titles. Cumulative publisher/personnel and subject indexes; a geographic one will be added. Entries are quite informative (even including citations for any articles published about the press) and many are not to be found in the standard directories. A few addresses are not current, but they should be updated in the next volume. Professional job, attractive and easy to read.

CCLM CATALOG OF LITERARY MAGAZINES.
1977. Coordinating Council of Literary Magazines, 80 Eighth Ave., NYC 10011. 55p. Loose-leaf binder edition free to libraries; bound edition to individuals for $.30 postage.

From the pink and silver cover to the spacious, easy to read format, a city slicker of a catalog listing 500 literary magazines by title (or, from *Abraxas* to *Zukunft*). Entries are rich: editor; address and telephone; type of material published; subscription information; date originally published; size of format and circulation. Geographical index too.

COSMEP/SOUTH,
Box 209, Carrboro, NC 27510.

Member presses strut their stuff in a free catalog. The quarterly newsletter ($5 year) gives news of conferences, distributors, publishers seeking manuscripts, new book notices. From the same address, get the *Cosmep Book Van Catalog* for a 9x12" self-addressed envelope with $.28 postage.

DIRECTORY OF SMALL MAGAZINE/PRESS EDITORS AND PUBLISHERS.
8th ed. 1977-78. Dustbooks, Box 100, Paradise, CA 95969. 184p. $6.95 (pbk); $21 for 4 year subscription to the annual.

Approximately 3600 names and addresses arranged alphabetically. The usual neat job by Dustbooks, foremost chronicler of the independent press.

DIRECTORY OF ETHNIC PUBLISHERS AND RESOURCE ORGANIZATIONS by Beth Shapiro.
1976, Michigan State University Libraries. From Office for Library Service to the Disadvantaged, American Library Association, 50 E. Huron St., Chicago 60611. 99p. $2.

An outgrowth of the vigilant SRRT Ethnic Materials Information Exchange Task Force. 289 publishers and groups, most dealing with Third World peoples, are listed with addresses and telephone; purpose of group; their publication titles and order information. Appendices on archival and research collections and distributors, with subject index.

FROM RADICAL LEFT TO EXTREME RIGHT by Theodore J. Spahn and Janet P. Spahn.
Volume 3, 2nd ed. 1976. Scarecrow Press. pp. 1001-1748. $22.50 (hdbk).

"Bibliography of current periodicals of protest, controversy, advocacy, or dissent, with dispassionate content-summaries." 474 signed reviews and 176 unsigned. Entries include price and frequency, format, when founded, circulation if available, description and feedback from the editor. The largest categories: Marxist-Socialist left, feminist, ethnic pride, metaphysical, radical left, liberal, gay liberation. Geographic, cumulative title, and editor/publisher/opinion indexes. Many of the periodicals have ceased or changed addresses so need verification, but offers a good historical record. Quality of reviews varies.

GUIDE TO ALTERNATIVE PERIODICALS by Don Carnahan.
2nd ed. 1977. From Sunspark Press, Box 91, Greenleaf, OR 97445. 69p. $3.

Over 670 U.S. magazines and journals which focus on "creative, constructive, nonwasteful lifestyles" are listed under 11 subject headings. An especially welcome consolidation of homesteading and natural living; spirituality and consciousness; health, nutrition and natural healing. Gives address and subscription data (though not rates for institutions), with a short description. Does not include alternative newspapers or literary magazines since these are documented elsewhere.

INTERNATIONAL DIRECTORY OF LITTLE MAGAZINES AND SMALL PRESSES by Len Fulton and Ellen Ferber.
13th ed. 1977-78. From Dustbooks, Box 100, Paradise, CA 95969. 440p. $11.95 (hdbk); $8.95 (pbk). 4-year subscriptions for $36 and $27.

There's nothing new to say about this classic except that it gets bigger every year and is *essential*! Fulton likens his work to "counting fry under a waterfall," with 700 new entries this year (the first edition in 1965 listed 250). Exhaustive magazine listings include editor, address and telephone, type of material used, subscription rates, average number of pages and other specifics about production and format, ad rates and discount schedules, etc. For presses, similar information including average press run and number of titles published for that year. 34p. subject index, index by state, list of 140 distributors and jobbers, and a helpful glossary of organization acronyms.

LEFT FACE: A Source Book of Radical Magazines, Presses, and Collectives Actively Involved in the Arts by Dan Georgakas.
1978, Cineaste Magazine and Smyrna Press. From Smyrna, Box 841, Stuyvesant Station, NYC 10009. 15p. $1.50.

Thirty-one publishers who describe themselves as anarchist, socialist or communist are listed with order information and a two-paragraph description (one each by compiler Georgakas and the group itself).

NEW PERIODICALS INDEX.
From The Mediaworks, Ltd., Box 4494, Boulder, CO 80306. Number 1 indexes Jan/June 1977. 143p. Semi-annual, $25/yr.

Primarily a subject index (author if major article) of 67 "alternative and new age" magazines, journals and newspapers. Not just articles, but columns, reviews of print, non-print, performances and art exhibits are indexed. Of the subject areas covered, the *Index* appears strongest in the arts, media, alternative technology and general radical news magazines (few of the major feminist periodicals are included). I'm glad someone is doing *Rain*, *Small Press Review* and others, but wouldn't call *Rolling Stone*, *Village Voice* and that ilk "alternative." A super-attractive and competent job.

SMALL PRESS RECORD OF BOOKS IN PRINT.
6th ed. 1977. From Dustbooks, Box 100, Paradise, CA 95969. 392p. $8.95 (pbk); $27 for 4-year subscription.

Not just books, but pamphlets, chapbooks, broadsides, posters and poem-cards from more than 700 publishers in the world. They are accessed by author, title, publisher, and subject by Len Fulton and his computer.

SOURCES: A Guide to Print and Nonprint Materials Available from Organizations, Industry, Government Agencies, and Specialized Publishers edited by Pat Schuman.
Neal-Schuman Publishers. From Gaylord Professional Publications, Box 61, Syracuse, NY 13201. Number 1, Winter 1977. 178p. 3x year/$60.

The first isssue lists 600 sources and more than 4000 titles (not with complete bibliographic information), followed by a title index, index to free and under $1.50 items, and cumulative subject index. For you vertical file freaks and resource compilers, Portland Cement or the Potato Board may not turn you on, but there are many alternative sources listed - it's a grab bag.

II. ALTERNATIVE REVIEW & NEWS MEDIA

AMERICAN BOOK NEWS,
Box 7458, Dallas, TX 75209. 10x, $5/year. Single copy $1.
 New tabloid from the publishers of the (also new) *Texas Arts Journal*. Reviews trade and university press books and some small press publications; useful columns on new magazines and authors/publishers. Seems to be aimed at the individual collector or literature freak with a tone somewhere between the academic and book trade journal.

AMERICAN BOOK REVIEW,
Box 188, Cooper Union Station, NYC 10003. Subscriptions: c/o Dept. of English, University of Colorado, Boulder, 80309. Bimonthly. $4/indiv.; $6/instit.
 A promising new 24-page tabloid reviewing "current books of literary interest published by the small, large, university, regional, third world, women's and other presses" for writers and the general public. One-page reviews mix the familiar (Fowles, Roth, Nin, Sexton) with Blue Wind, Tuumba and Unicorn Presses, Fiction Collective, etc. Reviewers in the first issue include Joyce Carol Oates, Ishmael Reed, Richard Kostelanetz and lesser known literati. Bill Henderson's column "Publishing As If" handily summarizes conglomerate trends and implications.

BOOKSWEST MAGAZINE,
3757 Wilshire Blvd., Los Angeles 90010. $15/12 issues.
 A West Coast version of *Publishers Weekly*, but with more content and less puffery. News of mergers and acquisitions, features on new technology in book production, profiles of small presses. Offers regular coverage of science fiction, mysteries, university presses and children's books, plus theme reviews of topic areas and round-ups like "Small Press Poetry." The short reviews include many independents and focus on paperbacks. Clair Peterson, former wizard of Bookpeople, adds zip with an "Editor's Choice" column.

CODA: Poets & Writers Newsletter.
Poets & Writers, Inc., 201 W. 54th St., NYC 10019. 5x year. $6/indiv.; $12/libraries (includes annual index volume). Single issue $1.50. Also publishes *Directory of American Fiction Writers* ($10 hdbk; $5 pbk) and *Directory of American Poets* ($3 pbk with free supplements).
 Money and survival concerns are uppermost-with news of taxes, grants and awards, agents, copyright, community arts funding. Think pieces are intriguing: will literary vouchers work?, does the alternative press publish fiction?, and an excellent summary of CCLM's campaign to woo library subscriptions ("Little Magazine Reader, Are You Out There?" Feb/March 1977). Attractive graphics, solid content, and a certain New York hustle.

COEVOLUTION QUARTERLY,
Box 428, Sausalito, CA 94965. Quarterly, $12 year. Single issue $3.50.
 Continues the *Whole Earth Catalog* in a magazine format. Research articles and interviews, short resource listings of books, magazines, bibliographies and tools dealing with land use, soft technology, understanding whole systems, etc. All this technology is leavened with tricks and treats by Dan O'Neill, Paul Krassner, Ken Kesey, Ursula Le Guin and other free spirits. Pulses with life and creativity. *CQ* also publishes a book series, maps and posters.

CONTACT II,
Eleven Broadway, Suite 933, NYC 10004. Bimonthly. $5/indiv.; $10/instit.

One year old, this poetry review is a folksy mixture of poetry, interviews and articles. Reviewers (poets, writers, teachers and community arts workers) write earnest reviews and generally avoid the infighting and cheap shrills. Tom Montag describes the continuum between one-person and large literary presses in "Small Press: Preliminary Notes Toward a Definition" in May 1977 issue.

COSMEP NEWSLETTER,
Box 703, San Francisco 94101. Monthly. Membership $25 for presses or associate members (non-publishers).

When you penetrate the dense type, you'll find a welter of news, reports of Cosmep conferences, controversies aplenty, regional reports, short articles on the business of getting reviewed and distributed, updates on projects like the book van and magazine racks in libraries, plus occasional reviews.

COSMEP PRISON PROJECT NEWSLETTER.
From Joseph and Carol Bruchac, The Greenfield Review, Greenfield Center, NY 12833. Sporadical, $2 year.

The project promotes communication between prisoners who write and editors and publishers. Newsletter contains articles and letters, listings of prison writing anthologies and books.

MARGINS.
From Star Distribution, Box 11609, Milwaukee 53211.

For years *Margins* passionately chronicled the small press, offering a rare forum for long reviews and serious consideration of new work by poets and writers. It finally became too much for its one-man band, Tom Montag. But back issues are still available. Number 8-27 except for 11, 19, and 23. Special focus numbers were: 12 (prison writing), 14 (grants), 20 (gay male writing), 21-22 (Latin American lit), 18 (Michael McClure symposium), 24-26 (Rochelle Owens). Montag's *Concern/s: Essays & Reviews 1972-1976* is also available from Star Distribution ($15 hdbk; $4.50 pbk). For libraries, an excellent resource is Tom Montag's article "Stalking the Little Magazine," *Serials Librarian*, Spring 1977, p. 281-303.

NEW MAGAZINE.
Published by Beyond Baroque Foundation, 1639 W..Washington Blvd., Venice, CA 90291. Foundation memberships and institutional subscriptions $15 (includes *Newforms* and *Newbooks*).

Poetry and short fiction, interviews and articles on the arts. Each issue has a theme such as poetry in the schools or film, but the main emphasis is on experimental writing. Literary news and events center on Southern California. Beyond Baroque operates a Small Press Library of 12,000 publications which is open to the public.

NEWSART.
From The Smith, 5 Beekman St., NYC 10038. Published twice a year as supplement to *The Smith* literary magazine. Subscription $8 year includes both.

Tasty tabloid of about 60 pages containing all manner of satire, expose, NY gossip, interviews, poetry, reviews of independent books and periodicals and the maddest letters. Sample article titles: "Writer Bites Gotham Rites," It's a Dog's Life section with "Bark Art" and "Dog Do Do Blues," "Beta-Days for Meta-Stories," "Witless in Naropa," etc.

NORTHEAST RISING SUN.
Cherry Valley Editions, Box 303, Cherry Valley, NY 13320. Sporadical, $8 year. Single issue $1.50.

Dynamic small press review which has progressed from an in-house affair to a panorama of avant contributors and topics. Profiles of presses, essays, collage, the information-packed "Small Press Scanner" and wicked articles like "The Great American Poetry Bake-Off, or, Why W. S. Merwin Wins All Those Prizes." Extensive reviewing and wrangling over books and periodicals by old hands like Hugh Fox. Style is rowdy and the North Beach male mystique lives, but there is good coverage of women writing too.

PACIFIC NORTHWEST REVIEW OF BOOKS.
Box 21566, Seattle 98111. Monthly. $7.50/indiv.; $9/instit.

This new 20-page tabloid review is very professionally done, but retains a refreshingly personal outlook, perhaps a rural brand of vigor and contemplation. Interviews with presses such as Pendragon and authors who live in the region, lengthy reviews of trade, university and independent presses with good coverage of Canadian publishing. Poetry, photographs, articles, and upcoming columns on Northwest literary history and bookstores.

RAIN: Journal of Appropriate Technology,
2270 N.W. Irving, Portland, OR 97210. 10x year, $10. Back issues $1. Requests no jobber orders.

"Access journal and reference service for people developing more satisfying patterns that increase self-reliance and press less heavily on our limited resources." Short *Whole Earth*-style listings of materials and groups dealing with energy, food ("peanut butter power"), transportation, etc.; solid technological updates, and philosophical pieces about lifestyles. *Rain* has evolved from a free newsletter to a trusted authority in the field of appropriate technology. Also publishes books and reprints of source lists.

RAINBOOK: Resources for Appropriate Technology.
1977. Shocken Books, 200 Madison Ave., NYC 10016. 251p. $15 (hdbk); $7.95 (pbk).

Includes most of the entries from *Rain* through the Feb/March 1977 issue, but not the articles. Supplies an introductory section and resource listings for everything from community building to waste recycling, with intriguing photos and illustrations. A thorough subject index too (*Rain*people are big on libraries as a source of "information power"). This is a beautiful book and reminiscent of that old favorite, *Place*.

SAN FRANCISCO REVIEW OF BOOKS,
2140 Vallejo St., San Francisco 94123. Monthly, $8 year. Single issue $.75

News, interviews, regular features "Western Spy," "Strictly San Francisco," and "Western Publishing." Reviews, both short and lengthy, of trade books with some university and small press titles. Regular columns on children's books, poetry, and a highlight, "The Book Arts," by fine printer Kathy Walkup. *SFRB* seems well on the way to becoming a useful recorder of the independent press scene and not just a sterile replica of the *New York Times Book Review*.

SMALL PRESS REVIEW.
Dustbooks, Box 100, Paradise, CA 95969. Monthly. $8/indiv.; $13.50/instit.

Part of the Len Fulton no-frills line, *SPR* was just ten years old. It contains Cosmep news, a continuing "Small Press Chronology," unannotated listings of all new books and magazines received, and short reviews by small press people. There are some focus issues (Oct-Nov 1977 on fiction problems and possibilities) and special articles like Ellen Ferber's "Quo Vadis" survey of editors and publishers (Jan-Feb 1977). Subscribers are automatically members of the Small Press Book Club (see p. 49).

WESTERN INDEPENDENT PUBLISHERS NEWSLETTER.
Box 31249, San Francisco 94131. Membership $10/year.

WIP is the product of a recent merger of Cosmep West and Literary Publishers of Southern California. The newsletter, by coordinator A.D. Winans, is full of plans for a warehouse and distribution system with a sales rep, and ongoing projects such as Small Press Racks in Libraries and combined mailing lists. Free catalog of WIP member publications is available. Winans is publishing *How To Raise the Dough*, a "grant seeker's bible" for the arts community (Second Coming Press, above address).

III. SELECTED DISTRIBUTORS

For additional sources, see *Alternatives in Print, Directory of Ethnic Publishers and Resource Organizations* and the *International Directory of Little Magazines and Small Presses*. For distributors of women's presses, see p. 62.

AKWESASNE NOTES,
Mohawk Nation, via Rooseveltown, NY 13683.

Akwesasne Notes, the advocacy newspaper of Native American peoples (5x year, for a donation), publishes books of poetry and politics, a "Six Nations Indian Museum Series" and a calendar. They also distribute many books on Native American culture and history, plus records and posters.

ATLANTIS DISTRIBUTORS,
Box 60119, New Orleans 70160.

A feminist collective distributing "life affirming books" about women, alternative technology, psychology and the occult, etc. The annotated mimeographed catalog offers a wide range of both trade and independently published books, calendars, and elusive periodicals.

BLACK BOX,
Box 4174, Washington, DC 20015.

Black Box, the first literary magazine in tape format, also produces cassette tape series of renowned and new poets. The Archive series preserves the voices of Berryman, Spicer, Reznikoff and others. Their Poet's Audio Center serves as a clearinghouse for cassette poetry available from commercial and noncommercial producers.

BOOK BUS,
c/o Visual Studies Workshop, 31 Prince St., Rochester, NY 14607.

The bus covers the New England area dealing small press publications (primarily literature and visual arts materials). The provocative catalog contains annotations, illustrations and photos of selections. Also available is a list of out of print photography books they carry.

BOOKPEOPLE,
2940 Seventh St., Berkeley, CA 94710.

Distributor to the book trade and libraries. Enticing and abundant stock of selected major and small press books. Established accounts receive their catalog and the small presses catalog twice a year plus the newsletter, *Bookpaper*, a brilliant bimonthly review.

CARRIER PIGEON,
88 Fisher Ave., Boston 02120.
 Distributor of radical and feminist books and magazines. A catalog, *Bookmarks*, features some of the materials on sexual politics, political economy, the Third World, etc.

COSMEP/SOUTH DISTRIBUTION,
Box 209, Carrboro, NC 27510.
 See p. 41.

ENERGY EARTH COMMUNICATIONS,
Box 8431, Southmore Station, Houston, TX 77004.
 Ahmos Zu-Bolton is the representative for this CCLM-funded regional bookstore distributor of small press materials.

LITERARY PRESS GROUP,
70 The Esplanade, 3rd Floor, Toronto, Ontario, Canada M5E 1R2.
 In a beautiful annotated catalog, the 23 Canadian member presses (Talonbooks, Coach House Press, Anansi) list works of fiction, drama, poetry and criticism by authors Jane Rule, Dorothy Livesay, etc.

NEW ENGLAND SMALL PRESS DISTRIBUTION,
45 Hillcrest Place, Amherst, MA 01002.
 A subsidiary of the New England Small Press Association, their spiral-bound catalog is $1. Some members are Magic Circle Press and periodicals *Antaeus*, *Chomo-Uri* and *Zahir Magazine*.

PLAINS DISTRIBUTION SERVICE, INC.,
Box 3112, Room 406, Block 6, 620 Main, Fargo, ND 58102.
 Distributor for Midwestern presses and selected magazines like *Margins* and *The Spirit that Moves Us*. The classy quarterly book lists describe works from Pentagram, Best Cellar, university presses, and more.

PRINTED MATTER, INC.,
7 Lispenard St., NYC 10013.
 Catalog of their unique collection of artists' books is $1.50.

QUARTO BOOK SERVICE,
Box 4727, Columbus, OH 43202.
 Handles contemporary poetry by mail order. Catalog lists virtually every poet, mingling university presses, the large trade publishers, the mediums (City Lights, Black Sparrow) and the littles (Alicejamesbooks, Ragnarok Press).

RAINBOW BRIDGE,
3548 22nd St., San Francisco 94114
 Full spectrum of religions including Spiritual Community, Ananda, and the occult.

RAYAS,
Box 7264, Albuquerque, NM 87104.
 A CCLM-funded "distribution cluster" for Chicano materials. They have produced a bibliography of Chicano writing, are developing a catalog and put out a newsletter. Jose Armas is the coordinator.

SELECT PRESS BOOK SERVICE,
14 South St., Milford, NH 03055.

Specializes in providing to libraries scholarly trade publications; those of associations, societies and museums; and most small presses. No journal or magazine subscriptions. The semi-annual *Select Press Review* is free to librarians.

SERENDIPITY BOOKS DISTRIBUTION,
1790 Shattuck Ave., Berkeley, CA 94709.

Distributes 50 selected presses and is exclusive distributor in the U.S. for about 1,000 poetry and prose titles. Some of the fine publishers represented in their catalog are Arif Press, Big Sky Books, Red Hill Press and back issues of *Caterpillar Magazine*.

SKYLO,
c/o The Book Project, 1502 East Olive Way, Seattle 98122.

Ivan Perry is the representative for this CCLM-funded regional bookstore distributor of small press materials.

SMALL PRESS BOOK CLUB,
Box 100, Paradise, CA 95969.

Quite different from the other 150 book clubs which tend to sleazy marketing and enforced book buying. Under a new structure, the only membership requirement for the Small Press Book Club is subscribing to the Small Press Review. (see p.46). The monthly selection list, received with SPR, offers a delightful mix of poetry, prose and periodicals. Take a chance with the "Alternative Press Packet" or the "Mag Bag." No titles published or distributed by Dustbooks will be included in the Book Club, or reviewed in SPR. Library memberships welcome.

SMALL PRESS TRAFFIC,
3841-B 24th St., San Francisco 94114.

Over 2,000 titles from 300+ presses are packed into this bookstore located in an old Victorian house. They do mail order, but don't have a complete catalog (there is a "West Coast Independent Presses" brochure).

SOUTHWEST LITERARY EXPRESS,
760 East Chestnut, Las Cruces, NM 88001.

David Apodaca is the representative for this CCLM-funded regional bookstore distributor of small press materials.

TRUCK DISTRIBUTION SERVICE,
1645 Portland Ave., St. Paul, MN 55104.

One of the most ambitious CCLM-funded distributors, offering 600 books from over 100 publishers and nearly 100 magazines. A helpful catalog supplies notes on publishers and book formats, how to simplify orders, etc. Stock includes the complete line of Black Sparrow, Coach House, and Plains Distribution Service, and a selected list from Serendipity. Turtle Island, Isthmus, Crossing Press and Manroot are just a few of the exciting publishers.

4.
FEMINISTS IN PRINT
by Valerie Wheat

The amazing multiplication of women's periodicals, publishers, distributors and bookstores can be seen as an expression of a blooming women's culture, and also as a part of the urge to take control of our lives. Just as women have begun to infiltrate the skilled trades, "male" professions such as the law, and higher corporate echelons, so they have penetrated publishing. Sure, women have always been employed in the publishing industry: as secretaries, ripped off editorial "assistants," in publicity and the school market, and in the nunnery of the children's book division. Unlike these women whose energy is diverted to battling tokenism and "working within the system," our energy (as well as the profit) goes into women owned and operated businesses. Women can perform all the jobs including editorial, typesetting, printing, binding, marketing, fiscal management and policymaking. Decisions are often made collectively and the cooperative structure replaces the hierarchy.

Having realized that information is power and that this society is media manipulated, we want to speak for ourselves. And if it seems that women's books are "accepted" now, that equal numbers will be published and reviewed, that's not the point. Only certain forms have received the imprimatur: the housewife-in-revolt novel, the how-to-get-yours guide for the woman executive, history or biography of women that is not too radical. But the men at the top make the decisions. Women may not be "publishable" (*i.e.*, profitable) tomorrow and it's off to the shredder. Examine some of the books and periodicals coming from the following publishers for another world light years ahead of the mass market. These books won't be advertised or reviewed so often or be as readily available in the local bookstore or library, but they are worth seeking out. What you see now will, in five years, perhaps be imitated and watered down into a "best seller."

I. GUIDES, DIRECTORIES, INDEXES

BIBLIOTECA FEMINA: A Herstory of Book Collections Concerning Women by Maryann Turner.
1977. 117p. From Maryann Turner, Box 251, Warrensburg, NY 12810. $5.

Part I is a chronological overview of the development of women's collections. Interesting historical material has been included such as the proposal for a World Center for Women's Archives in 1935. Of the 72 collections listed, the author has visited most or corresponded at length with the staff. Part II is an impressive proposal for creating a collection for the Mid-Hudson region of New York that could be adapted for any area. Full details are given on materials and staff, sample classification codes and catalog cards, estimates of task hours and costs. Warning: you may end up with an airline ticket and an itinerary of collections to explore for your own dream research project.

DIRECTORY OF WOMEN WRITING edited by Andrea Chesman and Polly Joan.
1977. Women Writing Press, RD 3, Newfield, NY 14867. 91p. $3.85.

Addresses and self-descriptions of 300 well-known and new writers with an additional mailing list of 600 writers and publications, arranged by state. The editors divined the need for a network when they published the popular *Women Writing Newsletter.* Interspersed with poems and drawings and bound in a glossy photo cover, the *Directory* is a lovely testament to Alta's observation on women writing: "we are legion."

FEMINIST RESOURCES FOR SCHOOLS AND COLLEGES: A Guide to Curricular Materials by Merle Froschl and Jane Williamson.
Rev. ed. 1977. Feminist Press, Box 334, Old Westbury, NY 11568. 67p. $2.95.

Comprehensive annotated bibliography of non-sexist books, pamphlets and articles for teachers and students from preschool through higher education, divided by subject. Sections on counselors and careers; guidelines and analysis of text and trade books; and Title IX are particularly welcome. Includes lists of periodicals, organizations and publishers.

FEMINIST WRITERS' GUILD.
Box 9396, Berkeley, CA 94709. Membership fee $10/indiv.; $5/unemployed; $20/feminist organizations, women's studies programs, etc.

This new national group is sprouting grassroots local chapters. Exciting plans for services include *The Feminist Writers' Handbook* ("how to get read and paid"); a file of feminist editors, agents and presses; eventual insurance and retirement plans. Also, agitation for political clout such as placing advertisements/protests in national literary and news magazines and organizing against discrimination by sexist media, distributors and grant-selection committees. Members receive the valuable *FWG Newsletter* three times a year.

GUIDE TO WOMEN'S PUBLISHING by Polly Joan and Andrea Chesman.
1978. Dustbooks, Box 100, Paradise, CA 95969. 296p. $9.95 (hdbk); $4.95 (pbk).

The compilers of the *Directory of Women Writing* have produced a wonderful new source book, obviously a labor of love. Annotated listings include 73 journals, 28 newspapers, 73 publishers, and printshops, non-sexist children's publishers, distributors, bookstores and other resources. In addition to these juicy entries, there are introductory essays to each section which discuss politics, problems with selection criteria, and document the development of women's publishing.

INDEX TO WOMEN'S MAGAZINES AND PRESSES by Charles Fishman.
1977. Seagull Publications, 1736 E. 53rd St., Brooklyn 11234. 22p. $2.

Intended to be a writer's guide to magazines and presses that publish women writers, but the listings were mostly lifted from *Writer's Market* and Dustbooks' directories without any follow-up. Most entries do not include an address and the description is so brief as to give no indication of the philosophy (for example, compare the entry for *Womanspirit* magazine with that in Lynne Shapiro's *Write On* for the difference first-hand knowledge makes). Plusses are lists of anthologies in progress and women's printshops, but one woman's bookstore?

MEDIA REPORT TO WOMEN INDEX/DIRECTORY edited by Martha Allen.
1978. From Women's Institute for Freedom of the Press, 3306 Ross Place, N.W., Washington, D.C. 20008. 59p. $8 (pbk).

Annotated index (by subject only) of the *Media Report to Women Newsletter*, see p. 56. Categories reflect the newsletter's broad scope spanning broadcast media, advertising, affirmative action, books, films, conferences, etc. The first index, cumulative for 1972-76, is available separately for $5.

The directory of women's media section (p. 17-42) supplies address, telephone and brief description for periodicals, distributors, and publishers; organizations and contacts in film, art, theatre, cable tv and libraries. There is no other such comprehensive and up-to-date source, particularly for the broadcast media (even lists woman-generated newspaper columns and radio shows). A 9-page list of individual mediawomen and addresses makes a useful mailing list.

NEW WOMAN'S SURVIVAL SOURCEBOOK edited by Kirsten Grimstad and Susan Rennie.
1975, Knopf. 245p. $5 (pbk).

This 11x14" Judy Chicago-covered catalog was a milestone in many ways: serious attention to women's information needs by a major publisher, the most ambitious national resource gathering combined with professional layout and graphics, and the distribution potential to reach many untouched women (probably some men too.) It is still a useful work, with sensitive introductory essays and interviews, though addresses for groups and publishers should be checked. The authors continue their information ovulation in *Chrysalis* (See Women's Periodicals).

ON EQUAL TERMS: A Thesaurus for Nonsexist Indexing and Cataloging compiled by Joan K. Marshall.
1977, Neal-Schuman Publishers. Distributed by ABC-Clio Press, Riviera Campus, 2040 APS, Box 4397, Santa Barbara, CA 93103. 152p. $14.95 (hdbk); $9.50 (pbk).

Marshall has toiled for years to liberate Library of Congress subject headings and to make women's materials more accessible through relevant indexing and language. This impressive volume should prove invaluable to workers classifying the chaotic garden of women's publications.

WOMEN AND LITERATURE: An Annotated Bibliography of Women Writers.
3rd ed. 1976. From Women and Literature Collective, Box 441, Cambridge, MA 02138. 212p. $3.80.

Capsule reviews of over 800 works of fiction, autobiography and literary criticism by women. The second edition sold 12,000+ copies in North America and Europe. This one has increased coverage of women workers and the labor movement, science fiction and mysteries. From cherished favorites to exciting discoveries, guaranteed to stimulate readers and some non-readers too.

WOMEN IN CALIFORNIA: A Guide to Organizations and Resources edited by Diana A. de Noyelles.
1977. From Center for California Public Affairs, Box 30, Claremont, CA 91711. 172p. $16.75 (pbk).

Comprehensive coverage of over 1600 governmental and community groups in 11 categories; especially useful are women's studies, health, education, work and money. Organization and subject indexes. Vital contacts from publishers and cultural centers to rape hotlines and career counseling.

WOMEN IN MEDIA: A Documentary Source Book by Maurine Beasley and Sheila Silver.
1977. Women's Institute for Freedom of the Press, 3306 Ross Place, N.W., Washington, DC 20008. 198p. $5.95.

A smashing collection of 30 articles spanning 1790 to the present which provide fascinating looks at colonial women printers, journalists from *Godey's Lady's Book* to war correspondents, and contemporary women in straight and movement media. Articles such as "Challenging Broadcast Licenses" detail legal challenges to discrimination. Worth the price alone is a personal account of the famous sit-in at the *Ladies Home Journal* in 1970.

WOMEN STUDIES ABSTRACTS edited by Sara Whaley.
Rush Publishing Co., Inc., Box 1, Rush, NY 14543. Quarterly. $20/indiv. prepaid; $25/libraries. Calendar year only. Single issue $4.50, $6.

After five years of struggling with the print explosion, Whaley recently announced price increases and changes in format. Over 50 abstracters cover articles, papers and reports relating to sex roles, employment, health, literature, etc. Annotations are expertly done and indexed by subject. Of special value are the bibliographic essay in each issue such as "Women in Hispanic Literature" and coverage of special issues of periodicals. Sources tend to the academic or professional media, not the "movement" periodicals covered elsewhere.

WOMEN'S INFORMATION SERVICES NETWORK DIRECTORY.
Contact Jen Felmley, Business & Professional Women's Foundation, 2012 Massachusetts Avenue, N.W., Washington, D.C. 20036. Forthcoming.

This directory will include all the libraries and resource centers which are members of the Women's Information Services Network founded at Wellesley College in 1975. They "provide information to and about women on a non-profit basis."

WRITE ON, WOMAN: A Writers' Guide to U.S. Women's/Feminist/Lesbian Alternate Press Periodicals by Lynne D. Shapiro.
From the author, 345 W. 87th St., NYC 10024. $3/indiv.; $4.25/instit.

Shapiro, a market researcher and NY radical feminist, published the guide in 1977 after sending out detailed questionnaires. It characterized 45 periodicals with how long and regularly been publishing, degree of interest in unsolicited manuscripts, circulation, type of payment, audience orientation, and deadlines. Titles were indexed by type of writing sought (reviews, excerpts from novels, etc.). A tremendously helpful tool, the first edition sold out. The new edition (available in July) includes 60 periodicals and newspapers, plus information on book publishers and graphic arts.

II. SELECTED FEMINIST REVIEW & NEWS MEDIA

Many more periodicals, creative writing journals, regional newspapers and newsletters exist. This list highlights national publications which regularly review the feminist presses. For other titles, check the directories listed previously such as *Write On, Woman* and *Guide to Women's Publishing.* A good resource for Canadian women's journals is *Emergency Librarian.*

CHRYSALIS,
c/o the Woman's Building, 1727 No. Spring St., Los Angeles 90012. Quarterly. $10/indiv.; $15/instit. Single issue $3.
 "Welcome to a magazine of women's culture." Theoretical articles and interviews that zap; transcendent fantasy, poetry and fiction; guerrilla collage and photos; Virgoesque resource lists, lengthy book reviews. And all the stars in the known feminist galaxy.

CONDITIONS,
Box 56, Van Brunt Station, Brooklyn 11215. 3x year. $6.50/indiv.; $10/instit. Single issue $2.50.
 Writing by women "with an emphasis on writing by lesbians." First issue is perfectbound, 142 pages of quality. Feature articles, an interview, fiction, poetry, a journal excerpt, list of publications received and numerous exquisite reviews of small press work including Audre Lorde, Mitsuye Yamada, books on battered women.

COUNTRY WOMEN,
Box 51, Albion, CA 95410. 5x year. $6/indiv.; $12/instit.
 A long-lived large circulation mag with intriguing mixture of creative writing, drawings and photos, reviews of trade and independent press materials, practical articles on sheep shearing or septic tank how-to. Issues center around a theme such as cycles, collectives, money.

FEMINIST ART JOURNAL,
41 Montgomery Place, Brooklyn 11215. Quarterly. Back issues $5 each.
 Cindy Nemser, editor of this quarterly devoted to women artists, past and present, has just announced that it will discontinue publication. Libraries should purchase back issues for the wealth of information and graphic records preserved.

FEMINIST BOOKSTORES NEWSLETTER edited by Carol Seajay.
c/o Old Wives Tales Bookstore, 532 Valencia, San Francisco 94110. Sporadical. Women-run, women-owned bookstores, distributors, publishers, and printers write for subscription rates; individuals $20 year. Send $1 for sample copy.
 Vital link in the Women In Print network. News of "the trade" (business, hassles, and highs) from bookstore owners; good grapevine on feminist and establishment publishing trends; reviews materials of interest to women. All women in print are enthusiastically invited to send in news, coups. Feminist publishers receive free mention of titles. Send in your lists! Other publishers, write for ad rates.

FEMINIST STUDIES,
Women's Studies Program, University of Maryland, College Park, MD 20742. Quarterly. $10/indiv.; $16/instit. Single issue $3; $4.50.
 Will resume publication with Volume 4 from a new home base. "Writing of a critical, scholarly, speculative and political nature which furthers feminist theory and consciousness."

HERESIES,
Box 766, Canal Street Station, NYC 10013. Quarterly. $11/indiv.; $16/instit. Single issue $3.

"Idea-oriented journal devoted to the examination of art and politics from a feminist perspective." Issues are focused, #3 was dynamite on "Lesbian Art and Artists." A definite New York City loft flavor, and the collective involves pioneers like Mary Beth Edelson, Miriam Schapiro, Joan Snyder, Susanna Torre. Provocative and stimulating, each issue takes days to mine.

MEDIA REPORT TO WOMEN,
3306 Ross Place, N.W., Washington, DC 20008. Monthly. $10/indiv. women prepaid; $15/other. Single issue $1.

Newsletter from Dr. Donna Allen who manages to keep up with the latest developments in publishing and broadcasting. Because of its frequency, the *Report* is a great source for new publications, address changes, governmental and foundation announcements. See also the *Media Report to Women Directory*.

OFF OUR BACKS,
1724 20th St., N.W., Washington, DC 20009. 11x year. $6/indiv.; $20/instit.

This newspaper has been going for seven years and continues to offer comprehensive coverage of women: international, court and prison cases, conferences and festivals, reviews of books, films and music. The letters and editorials keep up a lively debate on the latest controversy, with a lot of lesbian input.

PLEXUS,
2600 Dwight Way, Room 209, Berkeley, CA 94704. Monthly, $10 prepaid.

Newspaper covering the Bay Area, but also the national women's scene. News and commentary on current issues such as the Bakke decision or efforts to halt the violence against women theme in the recording industry. Regular column by Alta, poetry, reviews of films, books and music concentrating on alternative productions.

QUEST,
Box 8843, Washington, DC 20003. Quarterly. $9/indiv.; $15/instit. Single issue $3.

Each issue usually has five or more articles, academic in style, on "feminist political analysis and ideological development," plus creative writing or interviews. In three years, a variety of themes have been addressed including race, class and culture; spirituality; leadership; and communication and control.

SIGNS.
University of Chicago Press, 5801 Ellis Ave., Chicago 60637. Quarterly. $15/indiv.; $20/instit. Single issue $4; $5.

"Journal of women in culture and society," scholarly and social sciences-oriented. Issues center around a theme such as "Women and National Development." Book reviews are usually of university press books. *Signs* is especially good for getting an international viewpoint.

SINISTER WISDOM,
Box 30541, Lincoln, NB 68503. 4 x year. $7.50/indiv. Single copy price varies.

"Journal of words and pictures for the lesbian imagination in all women." Articles, poetry, fiction, constant dialogue between editors, authors and readers on the craft and politics of writing. Special issue #2($2.50) on "Lesbian Writing and Publishing" edited by Beth Hodges is a bonanza. Home grown in the best sense, meaning you don't have to have slick paper to publish Audre Lorde, Joanna Russ, etc. Graphics, too - you can get the electric photo cover/poster by Tee Corinne for $3.50.

WIN NEWS (Women's International Network).
187 Grant St., Lexington, MA 02173. Quarterly. $15/indiv.; $25/instit.

Incredibly rich news service reporting news of women, organizations and publications, from around the world (Africa, Middle East, Asia, Latin and North America, Europe). Sample topics: the U.N., health, violence, environment. Information you won't find elsewhere, for example, a bibliography on female circumcision.

WOMANSPIRIT,
Box 263, Wolf Creek, OR 97497. Quarterly. $6/indiv.; $10/instit. Single issue $2.

Produced by a collective process, this magazine is like a peek at a personal journal. Combines articles on witchcraft, healing and spiritual experience with poetry, revelations, original and startling photographs and drawings and book reviews.

WOMEN ARTISTS NEWSLETTER,
Box 3304, Grand Central Station, NYC 10017. 10x year. $5/indiv.; $6/instit.

Calendar of events, news and reviews of exhibitions, organizations, caucuses and conventions. Also book reviews and brief notes on publications. The critiques are hard-nosed; just because it's by a woman, it may not be good. Intelligently written and edited.

WOMEN'S STUDIES NEWSLETTER.
Feminist Press, Box 334, Old Westbury, NY 11568. Quarterly. $7/indiv.; $12/instit.

Joint publication with the recently formed National Women's Studies Association. News and task force reports, bibliographies, reviews of books and other curriculum aids, listings of conferences and jobs, personal experiences teaching women's studies.

III. FEMINIST BOOK PUBLISHERS

The following publishing houses (homes?) and collectives are owned and operated by women. The list does not include women or organizations who publish solely their own work. The best source for such fugitive publications is Women in Distribution (see Women Distributors, p. 62). Also not included are independent presses such as Capra and Crossing which publish many quality books by women. Such publishers can be located through the *International Directory of Little Magazines and Small Presses* and Bookpeople distributors. *Chrysalis* (see Women's Review Journals) has published guides to feminist publishing in issues 2 and 3 and plans future updates.

ALICEJAMESBOOKS,
138 Mt. Auburn St., Cambridge, MA 02138.

Writers' cooperative publishing poetry by women and a few men, notable not only for content but for first class book production and design.

ARTISTS & ALCHEMISTS,
215 Bridgeway, Sausalito, CA 94965.

If you're familiar with Adele Aldridge's concrete *Notpoems,* imagine what she might do as a publisher. For a start, *Erotica,* a woman's fantasy by Donna Ippolito.

WOMEN WORKING

BLUESTOCKING BOOKS,
Box 475, Guerneville, CA 95446.

Gina Covina and Laurel Holliday, of *Amazon Quarterly* fame, have formed this new house to publish quality paperbacks. Their first two titles are *Heart Songs: The Intimate Diaries of Young Girls* and *The Violent Sex: Male Psychology and the Evolution of Consciousness.*

BOOKLEGGER PRESS,
555 29th St., San Francisco 94131.

Current titles focus on film: *Women's Films in Print* and *Positive Images: Non-Sexist Films for Young People.* Scheduled this year is the stomping sequel to the old campaigner *Revolting Librarians,* as well as *The Anarcha-Feminist Papers.* We would also like to work on a second Women In Print Conference, and invite interested feminists to contact us.

DAUGHTERS, INC.,
MS590 P.O. Box 42999, Houston, TX 77042

The high roller of feminist publishing, Daughters was in the news for sale of mass market rights to Rita Mae Brown's *Rubyfruit Jungle.* They publish novels by women exclusively. Some of the more innovative authors are Bertha Harris, June Arnold and Monique Wittig.

DIANA PRESS,
4400 Market St., Oakland, CA 94608.

Diana now has the equipment and womanpower to take a manuscript in-house from editorial and artwork through printing, binding and distribution. In their catalog are many fine books of women's poetry, prose and lesbian herstory; new editions of searing Women's Press Collective poetry books by Pat Parker and Judy Grahn; and the forthcoming *Female Principle* by Elizabeth Gould Davis.

DOWN THERE PRESS,
Box 2086, Burlingame, CA 94010.

Publisher Joani Blank gets the "Clits-Up Award" for her loving books. First there were sex playbooks, then a buzz-o-rama guide to vibrators. Just out is the sumptously photographed *I Am My Lover,* a garden of self-delight.

DRUID HEIGHTS BOOKS,
685 Camino Del Canyon, Muir Woods, Mill Valley, CA 94941.

Elsa Gidlow has lived her life in advance of the trends, dropping out, coming out, etc. Publications include *Sapphic Songs: Seventeen to Seventy* and *Ask No Man Pardon: The Philosophical Significance of Being Lesbian.*

EFFIE'S PRESS,
1420 45th St., Studio 45, Emeryville, CA 94608.

Printer and designer Bonnie Carpenter creates beautiful letterpress books, and not at collector's prices. Mary Mackey's sassy poems sizzle in an orange neon cover while Adrienne Rich or Susan Griffin's work is wreathed in elegant leaf and vine motif.

FEMINIST PRESS,
Box 334, Old Westbury, NY 11568.

One of the foremothers of women's publishing, as well as women's studies. The press began by publishing reprints of women's stories and essays. Now they produce a wide variety of curricular materials (elementary through higher education) and biography and analysis ranging from Agnes Smedley to Nancy Drew to Kathë Kollwitz.

KELSEY STREET PRESS,
2824 Kelsey St., Berkeley, CA 94705.

This collective publishes poetry and anthologies of work by women poets and artists, including the kinky *Hair-Raising* in which the symbols and rites of hair are explored.

KNOW, INC.,
Box 86031, Pittsburgh 15221.

Another tried and true trailblazer, KNOW dared to publish the pamphlets and articles which shaped the women's liberation movement and fueled many a C-R group. Now that women's issues are "in," they continue to offer a back list of classic pamphlets, articles and bibliographies and have just published a new series of poetry books. Membership in KNOW ($6/indiv.; $10/instit.) brings the bimonthly *KNOW News Bulletin*.

LES FEMMES PUBLISHING,
231 Adrian Rd., Millbrae, CA 94030.

A subsidiary of Celestial Arts, a male-run publisher whose stock in trade is schlock (the inner yoga of frisbee genre). While some of this does rub off, Les Femmes has published a responsible "Everywoman's Guide" series and the important, but bleak *Proceedings of the International Tribunal on Crimes Against Women*.

MAGIC CIRCLE PRESS,
10 Hyde Ridge Rd., Weston, CT 06880. Distributed by Walker and Co., 720 Fifth Ave., NYC 10019.

The press has gone beyond celebrating Anais Nin to publish a novel by a new author, poetry by women in prison, and Valerie Harms' *Stars in My Sky* about Maria Montessori, Frances Steloff, and of course, Anais Nin. Quality books creatively designed.

MOON BOOKS,
Box 9223, Berkeley, CA 94709. Distributed by Random House (hardbacks) and Women in Distribution (paperbacks).

Anne Kent Rush, author of *Getting Clear*, began Moon Books to "increase the availability of a wider variety of fine feminist books in the general market." Titles have included her spirited *Moon Moon*, Dorothy Bryant's *The Kin of Ata*, *The New Lesbians* by the editors of *Amazon Quarterly*, and a fine history, *The Great Sioux Nation*.

MOTHEROOT PUBLICATIONS,
214 Dewey St., Pittsburgh 15218.

A new press started by Anne Pride (one of the founders of KNOW, Inc.) dedicated to publishing work by women "combining the art and politics inherent in the female experience." First publication is Adrienne Rich's pamphlet *Women and Honor: Some Notes on Lying*. A review mag for feminist press books is coming. Goddesspeed!

NAIAD PRESS, INC.,
20 Rue Jacob Acres, Bates City, MO 64011.

Publishes lesbian literature and attempts to preserve the heritage of the past as in translations of poetry and a novel by Renee Vivien. An anthology of book reviews by Barbara Grier (Gene Damon) from *The Ladder* and a bibliography on the lesbian in literature are steps in this documentation.

NEW WOMAN PRESS,
Box 56, Wolf Creek, OR 97497.

A partnership formed by Ruth and Jean Mountaingrove of *Womanspirit* magazine. Offerings include the *Turned On Woman Songbook*, cassette tapes of Ruth's songs, and an illustrated long biographical poem *For Those Who Cannot Sleep*.

NORTHWEST MATRIX,
1628 E. 19th Ave., Eugene, OR 97403.

Publishes feminist history, biography and politics including M.F. Beal's controversial account of the SLA, *Safe House*. Also distributes selected works from other presses such as *The Godfathers* by Naomi Weisstein (best known for her "Kinder, Kuche, Kirche As Scientific Law").

OUT & OUT BOOKS,
476 2nd St., Brooklyn 11215.

Primarily poetry: the old standby anthology *Amazon Poetry* which contains work by most of the lesbian celebs; individual collections by NY poets like Jan Clausen and Joan Larkin; and several books "with anger and love" from the more political Susan Sherman.

PEARLCHILD PRODUCTIONS,
Distributed by WIND, Box 8858, Washington D.C. 20003.

Tee Corinne's *Cunt Coloring Book* continues to creme crayolas, with Pat Califia's *Sapphistry: A Lesbian Sexuality Workbook* soon to cummmmmm.

PERSEPHONE PRESS: A Branch of Pomegranate Productions,
Box 7222, Watertown, MA 02172.

For a unique experience, try the revolutionary *Feminist Tarot* by Sally Gearhart and Susan Rennie or the *Pricella Pumps-Starbuckwheat Comic Book*.

SHAMELESS HUSSY PRESS,
Box 3092, Berkeley, CA 94703.

Her books have evolved from early home-printed cheapies to perfectbound, but Alta continues to challenge the conventional. An impressive record includes early publication of Susan Griffin, pre-Broadway Ntozake Shange; and the reprint *Calamity Jane's Letters*.

SUNBURY PRESS,
Box 274, Jerome Ave. Station, Bronx, NY 10468.

Publishes *Sunbury* poetry magazine and chapbooks by publisher Virginia Scott, Kathleen Meagher, and Lorraine Sutton's Latin beat *SAYcred LAYdy*.

VANITY PRESS,
Box 15064, Atlanta, GA 30333.

Published poetry and a novel by Sonya Jones and short stories of lesbian life by Hadden Luce.

VIOLET PRESS,
Box 398, NYC 10009.

Lesbian poetry in anthology, *We Are All Lesbians*, and individual books by Judy Greenspan and Fran Winant. *Dyke Jacket* is Winant in top political/mythical form as in "Eat Rice Have Faith in Women."

WOMANPRESS,
Box 59330, Chicago 60645.

Marie Kuda compiled the annotated bibliography *Women Loving Women* for a Lesbian Writers Conference. Other publications are an anthology generated at a conference and poetry by Jeanette Foster and Valerie Taylor, legendary figures in lesbian lit.

WOMANSHARE BOOKS,
Box 1735, Grants Pass, OR 97526.

In *Country Lesbians*, the five women who make up the WomanShare collective discuss living off the land in terms of physical, spiritual and financial survival.

WOMEN WRITING PRESS,
RD 3, Newfield, NY 14867.

Have published two dedicated poets, Polly Joan (*No Apologies*) and Alison Colbert (*Let the Circle Be Unbroken*). Also, the *Directory of Women Writing* (see

WOMEN'S PRESS,
280 Bloor St. West, Suite 313, Toronto, Ontario, Canada. Distributed in the U.S. by Bookpeople.

It's hard to choose from the many fascinating titles they publish: *A Harvest Yet to Reap: History of Prairie Women, Anti-Psychiatry Bibliography, Women at Work*, and other books and pamphlets on women and work and the social history of Canada. See their entry under Kids' Liberated Literature.

WOMEN WRITING by The Great Atlantic Radio Conspiracy.
1976. GARC, 2743 Maryland Ave., Baltimore 21218. ½ hour audio-cassette, $3.50.

Inspiring interviews with the publishers of *Women: A Journal of Liberation, 13th Moon*, Daughters, and KNOW. You hear their enormous energy and commitment against all odds, backed with woman music, and the GARC's traditional sign-off takes on its full meaning: "Watch your step. You may become part of the Conspiracy."

IV. DISTRIBUTORS OF FEMINIST MATERIALS

ALICE B'S BOOKSERVICE,
Box 4190, Berkeley, CA 94704.

Specializes in out-of-print lesbiana and women's studies literature. Catalog $1 and will perform title searches.

AMAZON REALITY,
Box 95, Eugene, OR 97401.

Revolutionary sex education manual for high school women; *Come Out Comix* and *What Lesbians Do*; books and pamphlets of poetry and politics; posters.

FEMINIST BOOK MART,
Box 149, Whitestone, NY 11357.

Non-sexist children's books; pamphlets and bibliographies on women's studies and curricula; general women's titles. Catalog.

KNOW, INC.,
Box 86031, Pittsburgh, PA 15221.

Pamphlets, reprints, books and bibliographies on every area of women's lives. Catalog. See entry under Women Publishers.

NANNY GOAT PRODUCTIONS,
Box 845, Laguna Beach, CA 92652.

Raunchy women's comics: *Tits & Clits*, *Wimmen's Comix # 1-7*, *Abortion Eve*, the ever-popular *Pudge*, and more.

OLD LADY BLUE JEANS,
200 Main St., Northampton, MA 01060.

Calendars, posters, and Elana Dykewoman's *They Shall Know Me By My Teeth*, poems that bite.

WIND (Women in Distribution, Inc.),
Box 8858, Washington, D.C. 20003. Bookstores and libraries only.

A real success story, they handle 400 books, records, and graphic items. Most of these are from independent publishers and the importance of this network to both publishers and buyers can't be overemphasized. The beautiful 52 page catalog is annotated and includes evocative photographs of women from the Library of Congress archives.

WOMAN'S PLACE BOOKSTORE,
5251 Broadway, Oakland, CA 94618.

One of the oldest women's bookstores, it carries a full selection of books, periodicals, pamphlets, records and children's books. Mail order on a limited basis - no catalog available.

5.
KIDS' LIBERATED LITERATURE
by Valerie Wheat

When feminists began examining reading, language and other school textbooks, they found things hadn't really changed much since their own relentless Dick and Jane Days (perhaps a few faces had been colored in for ethnicity). Turning to picture and preschool books, they found a similarly stereotyped world where girls were onlookers, reflecting the limited roles and aspirations of women in society. To create new stories and pictures women began to publish. There was much to learn, and some of the first books were heavy-handed in their ideology, simply not high interest stories, or flimsily produced. Today, these publishers are turning out fine work. New research is being done on folk tales and legends involving females, and word has spread to teachers, parents, and librarians looking for depictions of active girl characters and themes that go beyond the sterile, white "typical" family with mom in her apron.

For reviews of books from some of the publishers listed here read Nancy Schimmel's "Kids and Libraries" column in *Booklegger Magazine*, issues #5-16. For news and reviews of the prolific Canadian sources, get *Emergency Librarian*.

ALL OF US, INC.,
Box 4552, Boulder, CO 80306.
This small collective has published *Mother Is a Pitcher* (on a baseball team), *Hooray For Ginger* and the bilingual *Zenaida*.

BEFORE WE ARE SIX,
12 Bridgeport Rd. East, Waterloo, Ontario, Canada. Distributed by Women's Press (see below).
Timely titles like *My Feet Roll* about two sisters, one of whom is disabled; and *The Last Visit* about the death of a grandmother. *Irene's Idea*, *Minoo's Family* and others deal with family situations that aren't "perfect."

CHILDREN'S BOOK PRESS,
1461 Ninth Ave., San Francisco 94122.
Fifth World Tales is a wonderful series of bilingual legends from Latin and South America and Puerto Rico illustrated in muralist style. A new series includes a Chinese legend *The Iron Moonhunter* and Vietnamese and Native American tales.

COUNCIL ON INTERRACIAL BOOKS FOR CHILDREN RESOURCE CENTER,
Room 300, 1841 Broadway, NYC 10023.

Publishes the *Bulletin* (8x year, $10/indiv.; $15/instit.) which analyzes materials for stereotypes and provides strategies to counteract them. Regular book review and media monitor sections. Double issues have focused on different ethnic groups, aging, and the handicapped.

CIBC publishes many books, pamphlets, classroom guides and non-print media which discuss racism and sexism and promote multicultural education.

FEMINIST PRESS,
Box 334, Old Westbury, NY 11568.
Published some of the very first non-sexist children's books. Classic titles are *Coleen the Question Girl* and *Firegirl*. Others include *Nothing But a Dog* and the English/Spanish *My Mother the Mail Carrier*.

JOYFUL WORLD PRESS,
468 Belvedere St., San Francisco 94117.

Shirley Boccaccio is probably most famous for her "Fuck Housework" poster, but she is also the author of the Penelope series. The latest one, *Penelope and the Earth*, has an ecological theme.

KIDS CAN PRESS,
Box 5974, Postal Station A, Toronto, Ontario, Canada.

Designed for urban children, *The Double Double Mirror* tells of a suddenly extended family and *Julie News* about a neighborhood crisis. Others are *I'm a Child of the City* and *The Christmas Tree House Tale*.

LEARN ME, INC.,
642 Grand Ave., St. Paul, MN 55105.

Bookstore with a mail order catalog offering an incredible array of books, picture books, puzzles, teaching aids and records on sex roles, career education, other cultures, etc.

LIBERTY CAP: A Catalog of Non-Sexist Materials for Children by Enid Davis.
Academy Press, Ltd., 176 W. Adams St., Chicago 60603. $4.95 (pbk).

Selected material from the bimonthly review journal *The Liberty Cap* (ceased publication in 1976) on non-stereotyped children's books, films and other media.

LOLLIPOP POWER,
Box 1171, Chapel Hill, NC 27514.

Lollipop was one of the first to present a new view of the world with *Martin's Father, Grownups Cry Too* and the curious penguin of *Carlotta and the Scientist*. *The Sheep Book* by Carmen Goodyear, of *Country Women* magazine, is non-fiction and *Amy and the Cloud Basket* a fable.

NEW SEED PRESS,
Box 3016, Stanford, CA 94305.

Their *A Book About Us* is a fun "publisher" story. Four kids write and illustrate a book about their own lives and then work with a women's print shop to get it published. *Peter Learns To Crochet*, *Fanshen the Magic Bear* solves a riddle, and *Some Things You Just Can't Do by Yourself*. The bilingual story, *La Aventura de Yolanda*, has been a hit.

OVER THE RAINBOW PRESS,
Box 7072, Berkeley, CA 94707.

A reversal of the standard rescue tale, *The Forest Princess* wakes the sleeping prince. Also by Harriet Herman, *The Return of the Forest Princess*. Posters are available for both books and a color filmstrip and cassette for *The Forest Princess*.

WOMEN'S PRESS,
280 Bloor St. West, Suite 313, Toronto, Ontario, Canada. Distributed in the U.S. by Bookpeople (see alternative distributors, Chapter 3).

Old timers *Mandy And The Flying Map* and the *Travels Of Ms. Beaver*. Good new titles are *Muktu: The Backward Muskox*, *I Climb Mountains* and *She Shoots! She Scores!* about Hilary the hockey player.

6.
THE LIBRARY FREE PRESS
by Valerie Wheat

An "alternative" library publishing explosion has happened in the last six years. *Synergy* lit a spark in the doldrums of library literature. *Booklegger* and *Emergency Librarian* carried on the flame. Now there are a number of more specialized publications aiming to fill the vacuum of what is not covered regularly, in depth, or with awareness by the established library media: women's publishing and resources, prison service, young adult service and issues, non-sexist children's resources, ethnic service and publishing, and responsible, non-racist cataloging. In short, the library profession is beginning to come into the 20th century, and, like other professions of law, medicine, social work and teaching, the more radical members seek alternatives. Commercial library journals already in existence are mired in coverage of ALA, articles by male administrators who lay down the law or show off their academic terminology, "non-biased" bland reviews of trade books, and non-recognition of the significance of independent publishing. At least half their pages are devoted to advertisements for the same trade books they "objectively" review.

The established library press currently gives a few nods to independent publishing (see "The Library Industrial Complex" listed on p. 34). In *Library Journal*, Bill Katz has put together a monthly "Magazines" column, and his annual "Small Press Round-up" used to mean life or death for an independent without access to the review/advertising circuit. American Library Association's *Booklist* features an irregular column "Alternative Press Scene" which is nicely done by Val Morehouse, and has run coverage of women's presses by Kay Cassell. *Wilson Library Bulletin* did have a regular "Alternative Periodicals" column by James Danky and Len Fulton of Dustbooks used to write a small press column for *American Libraries*, but it disappeared and was not replaced.

For regular, committed and lively coverage of the independent press and the library profession, check out the following. They are especially important for library school students who need affirmation, humor and support. But, unfortunately, many library school libraries do not collect these publications and are not even aware of their existence. No one can live by *Library Qvarterly* alone!

BOOKLEGGER MAGAZINE.
555 29th St., San Francisco 94131. Sporadical, $3/issue. Back issues #1-16 (except for #3/4) available for $2 each.

Our magazine will reincarnate as *The Feminist Review of Books* if the weather's good (i.e., jucier toons when we can pay the piper). Until then, we will do "sporadicals" for librarians and bookworkers on the media software you love to touch.

If you haven't seen previous focus issues #5 "Librarians and Publishers" or #13 "Library Schools," you'll be sorry because they are going out of print years ahead of their time. Other issues are full of resource lists on such things as Madness, Menstruation, Class, Cooperative Housing, etc.; reviews of the independent press; columns on kids and media.

COLLECTORS' NETWORK NEWS.
From James P. Danky, Editor, State Historical Society of Wisconsin, 816 State St., Madison, WI 53706. Bimonthly, $6 year. Single issue $1.

The successor to Russ Benedict's feisty *Top Secret* newsletter is aimed at librarians who acquire and process alternative and extremist periodicals. Contains reviews, updates on cataloging, histories of collections like the Alternative Press Centre, and bibliographies. Future topics: political lit of the Caribbean, food coop and health rights publications, Defense Dept. periodical lit, etc.

EMERGENCY LIBRARIAN.
c/o Sherrill Cheda, 46 Gormley Ave., Toronto, Ontario, Canada M4V 1Z1. Bimonthly. U.S. $9/indiv.; $12, instit. Canada $7 and $10. Student/$3.

This excellent journal now boasts a nifty typeset format with tasteful graphics. Resource articles, reviews of print and non-print materials from Canada and the U.S. Frank analysis of issues in Canadian librarianship such as the status of women and non-professionals, and the role of CLA. Particularly good coverage of women's presses and a superb "books for liberated kids" section. Focus issues have included the law, technical services, feminist publishing.

HENNEPIN COUNTY LIBRARY CATALOGING BULLETIN.
Technical Services Division, Hennepin Co. Library, 7001 York Ave. South, Edina, MN 55435. Bimonthly. $6/indiv.; $12/instit. Back issues $1.50.

Sandy Berman foments and documents The Cataloging Revolution. Detailed lists of Hennepin County Library additions and revisions to the imperial Library of Congress system with explanatory notes and suggested subject headings for controversial topics dealing with race, religion, sexuality. An "Added Entry" section airs the complaints and whimsical visions of catalogers. Also publishes a quarterly *Authority File* in microfiche.

INSIDE/OUTSIDE: A Newsletter on Library Services to Youth and Adults in Prisons, Jails, and Detention Centers.
Box 9083, Berkeley, CA 94709. Quarterly. $3.50/prepaid; $5/if billed.

Begun in 1974 by jail service librarians Joan Ariel and Gilda Turitz, *IO* has developed an enthusiastic readership. Contributors exchange information on new publications, creative writing programs, legal developments and censorship hassles, techniques of dealing with the juvenile justice system.

LIBRARIANS FOR SOCIAL CHANGE.
From John L. Noyce, Box 450, Brighton, Sussex, U.K. BN1 8GR. 3x year. U.S. libraries $10; indiv. $4. Single copy $3; $1.

"Forum for the reappraisal of methods of getting information to the people." Short radical articles on libraries "after the revolution," left wing libraries in England, sexism in children's books, the politics of information. Letters, book reviews, bibliographies, occasional indexing of the alternative press, and the latest proof of the "irrelevancy of the Library Association." Minimal attention to format (mimeographed), but the content is gutsy and refreshing.

From the same address Noyce (formerly Smoothie Publications) publishes pamphlets and bibliographies on alternative technology, censorship in libraries and social history. Noyce's *Directory of Alternative Periodicals* will be available early in 1978 from Harvester Press, 2 Stanford Terrace, Hassocks, Sussex.

ROCKING CHAIR.
From Cupola Productions, Box 27, Philadelphia 19105. Monthly. $9.85/librarians; $11.85/non-library. Single issue $.90 and $1.

"Review newsletter for librarians and popular music fans who buy records." Rates and reviews rock, country, reggae, anything but classical or jazz. Also covers record care, recommended sheet music, reference questions and answers, selective discographies (Elvis, Bing, Latin America) and book reviews. A handy source, especially for young adult librarians. Reviews are knowledgeable and interesting.

SRRT NEWSLETTER (Social Responsibilities Roundtable of the American Library Association).
SRRT Clearinghouse, 60 Remsen St., #10E, Brooklyn 11201. Bimonthly. $5/ALA member; $3/non-ALA; $20/instit. Back issues $1.

The fold-out format is cumbersome, but there's news of SRRT affiliates and task force activities, pre and post-convention strategies and politics, letters and brief notes on social change publications.

SIPAPU.
From Noel Peattie, Rt. 1, Box 216, Winters, CA 95964. 2x year, $4.

"Newsletter for librarians, editors, collectors, and others interested in alternative publications, including third world, dissent, feminist, self-reliant and underground publications." A collage of interviews, reviews, eyewitness reports from conventions and publishing conferences. Noel's nose for petite detail and Jane Austenian sensibility make *Sipapu* unique.

He also operates the Cosmep "Civil Sayings Project" which will send a free packet of poetry broadsides to any library on request.

SYNERGY, 1967-1973.
Published by the Bay Area Reference Center, San Francisco Public Library; edited by Celeste West. Sets available from Booklegger Press.

The Mother of The Library Free Press, cream of the dream 60's. Now out of print, but original issues (#1-42) available from us. Expensive, but what isn't. Write for quotes.

TITLE VARIES,
Box 704, Chapel Hill, NC 27514. Sporadical. $5/prepaid; $6/if billed. On calendar year basis only. Single issue $1.

The surreal world of serials librarians "united to fight costly, silly, unnecessary serial title changes." List of title changes, the serials scene at library conventions, how to deal with Ebsco and Faxon, and relevant book reviews. The long-suffering librarians keep their wit about them by concocting Title Change Awards like "the territorial imperative" (the *Kansas Journal of Sociology* became the *Mid-American Review of Sociology*) and "the deep significance." One of the worst offenders was the *Quarterly Economic Review: Italy* changed to *QER: Italy* to *Quarterly Economic Review of Italy* in a series covering 100 different countries/titles.

UNABASHED LIBRARIAN,
G.P.O. Box 2631, NYC 10001. Quarterly, $10 year. Back issues $2.50.

The "how I run my library good" letter, now being emulated by *Library Journal.* Editor Marvin Scilken provides a valuable service by abstracting the rare jewel from *Business Week,* Library of Congress and governmental bulletins, etc. Readers also submit ideas for cataloging, processing, and publicizing library materials; bibliographies and filmographies on trendy topics; and brief reviews. It's an intrepid hodgepodge with humor and the urge to demystify. Also published *Go, Pep, and Pop!: 250 Test Ideas for Lively Libraries.*

VOICE OF YOUTH ADVOCATES.
From Dorothy M. Broderick, 111 South Highland Ave., Apt. 3, Ossining, NY 10562. Bimonthly. $10 year; $11/if billed.

A new "magazine for librarians working with junior/senior high school age youth in schools, public libraries and institutions." Edited and published by two irrepressible YA advocates, Mary K. Chelton and Dorothy Broderick. Features include "In the I&R Corner"; reviews of mysteries, pop records, science fiction, general adult fiction and nonfiction; and special attention to original paperbacks, pamphlets, films for programming and professional materials from librarianship and related disciplines.

WOMEN IN LIBRARIES,
Newsletter of the ALA/SRRT Task Force on Women. From Kay Cassell, Bethlehem Terrace, Apt. H-181, Slingerlands, NY 12159. 5x year. $4/indiv.; $6/instit.; $1/student or unemployed.

News of ALA actions and programs concerning women, and of SRRT Task Force projects. Essential notes on the latest publications about women, continuing education programs for women in management, legal actions, and much more.

WOMEN LIBRARY WORKERS,
Newsletter of Women Library Workers. From WLW, Box 9052, Berkeley, CA 94709. Bimonthly. $10/WLW membership; $5/newsletter to institutions and non-members.

Offers a forum for members to communicate on WLW structure and what issues will be considered (problems of special librarians, job sharing, pay parity, unions, relation between professional and non-professional library workers). News of local chapter actions, notes on women in publishing and members' doings. Neat and attractive in appearance, sisterly and assertive in style.

WLW also publishes the unique *SHARE (Sisters Have Resources Everywhere) Directory* of feminist library workers. The third edition will be available soon.

YOUNG ADULT ALTERNATIVE NEWSLETTER.
From Carol Starr, 37167 Mission Blvd., Fremont, CA 94536. 5x year. $4/prepaid; $4.50/ if billed.

News of library conferences and Young Adult Services Division, strategy for getting administration and budget behind YA services, ideas for programs and publicity, "random notes" on print and non-print materials, and heart to heart letters. Big issues are sex, YA selection standards, counseling and confidentiality. Exudes that old YA enthusiasm and spacyness; April Fool issue carried a hilarious spoof, *YAWN* (Young Adult Workers Newsletter).

INDEX: To Titles & Organizations

A
- "About Books"   34
- Akwesasne Notes   47
- Alice B's Bookservice   62
- Alice James Books   57
- All of Us, Inc.   65
- Alternative Press Index   40
- Alternatives In Print   34, 40
- Alternatives (Univ. Of CT)   40
- Amazon Reality   62
- American Book News   34, 43
- American Book Review   34, 43
- American Libraries Magazine   34
- American Odyssey   33
- Art & Science of Book Publishing   30
- Artists & Alchemists   57
- Association of American Publishers   31
- Atlantis Distributors   47

B
- Before We Are Six   65
- Biblioteca Femina   52
- Black Box   47
- Bluestocking Books   59
- Book Bus   47
- Book Manufacturers' Institute   36
- Book Production Industry Magazine   26
- Book Publishers Directory   40
- Book Publishing: What It Is   22
- Booklegger Magazine   70
- Booklegger Press   59
- Booklist Magazine   34
- Bookmaking   26
- Bookpeople   47
- Books: From Writer To Reader   22
- Books In Print   34
- Bookswest Magazine   34, 43
- Business of Publishing   22

C
- Cal-Syl Press   24
- Candid Critique of Book Publishing   23
- Carrier Pigeon   48
- Cataloging In Publication   23
- CCLM Catalog of Literary Magazines   41
- Children's Book Press   66
- Choice Magazine   34
- Chrysalis Magazine   55
- Coda: Poets & Writers Newsletter   43
- Coevolution Quarterly   43
- Collectors' Network News   70
- Conditions Magazine   55
- Contact II Magazine   45
- Co-op Publishing Handbook   23
- Copyright Information   23
- COSMEP Newsletter   23, 45
- COSMEP Prison Project Newsletter   45
- COSMEP/South   41
- COSMEP/South Distribution   48
- Council on Interracial Books For Children   66
- Country Women Magazine   55
- Cumulative Book Index   34

D
- Daughters, Inc.   59
- Denver Publishing Institute   36
- Design of Books   27
- Diana Press   59
- Directory of Ethnic Publishers   41
- Directory of Small Magazine/Press Editors & Publishers   41
- Directory of Women Writing   52
- Down There Press   59
- Druid Heights Books   59

E Editing By Design   27
Edwards Brothers   24
Effie's Press   59
Emergency Librarian   70
Energy Earth Communications   48

F Feminist Art Journal   55
Feminist Book Mart   62
Feminist Bookstores Newsletter   55
Feminist Press   59, 66
Feminist Resources for Schools & Colleges   52
Feminist Studies   55
Feminist Writers' Guild   52
Fine Print   27
Forecast Magazine   34
From Cover To Cover   27
From Radical Left To Extreme Right   41

G Guide To Alternative Periodicals   41
Guide To Women's Publishing   52

H Hennepin County Cataloging Bulletin   70
Heresies Magazine   56
Horn Book Magazine   34
How To Be Your Own Publisher   24
How To Do Leaflets, Newsletters, & Newspapers   27
How To Get Happily Published   24
How To Publish Information   27
How To Publish, Promote, & Sell Your Book   25
How To Self-Publish Your Own Book & Make It A Bestseller   33
Huenefeld Guide To Book Publishing   31
Huenefeld Report   24

I Index To Women's Magazines & Presses   53
Inside/Outside Newsletter   70
International Directory of Little Magazines & Small Presses   34, 42
Into Print   25
Introduction To Design Poetics   27

J Joyful World Press   66

K Kelsey Street Press   60
Kids Can Press   66
Kirkus Reviews   34
KNOW, Inc.   60, 62

L Learn Me, Inc.   66
Left Face   42
Les Femmes Publishing   60

Liberty Cap   66
Librarians For Social Change   70
Library Journal   34
Literary Market Place   25
Literary Press Group   48
Lithographer 3 & 2   28
Lollipop Power   66

M Magic Circle Press   60
Margins   45
Media Report To Women Index/Directory   53
Media Report To Women Newsletter   56
Moon Books   60
Motheroot Publications   60

N Naiad Press   60
Nanny Goat Productions   63
New England Small Press Distribution   48
New Magazine   45
New Periodicals Index   42
New Seed Press   67
New Woman Press   60
New Woman's Survival Sourcebook   53
New York Review of Books   35
New York Times Book Review   35
New York University: "Book Publishing"   37
Newsart   45
Northeast Rising Sun   46
Northwest Matrix   61

O Off Our Backs   56
Offset-Graphics, Printing, Binding   28
Old Lady Blue Jeans   63
On Equal Terms   53
One Book/Five Ways   25
Out & Out Books   61
Over The Rainbow Press   67

P Pacific Northwest Review of Books   46
Pearlchild Productions   61
Persephone Press   61
Plains Distribution Service   48
Plexus   56
Pocket Pal   28
Postal Service Manual   31
Pride Program   28
Printed Matter, Inc.   48
Printing For The Movement   28
Printing It   28
Printing Types   28
Publicizing Your Self-Published Book   33
Publish It Yourself Handbook   25
Publishers Weekly   25, 31, 32, 35
Publishing: The Creative Business   31

Q Quatro Book Service   49
Quest   6, 56

R Radcliffe Publishing Course   37
Rain   46
Rainbook   46
Rainbow Bridge   48
Rayas   48
Real Paper   35
Rochester Institute of Technology   37
Rockingchair   71
Rooms With No View   6

S San Francisco Review of Books   35, 46
Sarah Lawrence "Publishing Laboratory"   37
Saturday Review   35
School Library Journal   35
Select Press Book Service   49
Select Press Review   35
Serendipity Books Distribution   49
Shameless Hussy Press   61
Signs Magazine   56
Sinister Wisdom Magazine   56
Sipapu   71
Skylo   49
Small Press Book Club   49
Small Press Record Of Books In Print   42
Small Press Review   35, 46
Small Press Traffic   48
Small-Time Operator   32
Soho Weekly News   35
Sources   42
Southwest Literary Express   49
SRRT Newsletter   71
Stanford Publishing Course   37
Sunbury Press   61
Synergy   71

T Title Varies   71
To Advance Knowledge   30
Truck Distribution Service   49

Typeworld Newspaper   29

U Ulrich's Periodical Directory   32
Unabashed Librarian   72

V Vanity Press   61
Village Voice   35
Violet Press   61
Voice of Youth Advocates   72

W Washington Post Book World   35
West Coast Review of Books   35
Western Independent Publishers Newsletter   47
Western Publishing Scene   35
Wilson Library Bulletin   35
WIN News   57
WIND (Women In Distribution, Inc.)   63
Womanpress   61
Woman's Place Bookstore   63
Womanshare Books   62
Womanspirit   57
Woman And Literature   53
Women Artists Newsletter   57
Women As Printers   29
Women In Libraries   72
Women In California   54
Women In Media   54
Women Library Workers   72
Women Studies Abstracts   54
Women Writing (cassette)   62
Women Writing Press   62
Women's Information Services Network Directory   54
Women's Press   62, 67
Women's Studies Newsletter   57
Write On, Woman!   54
Writer Publisher   33
Writer's Guide To Book Publishing   26

Y Young Adult Alternative Newsletter   72

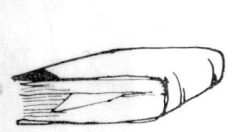   

Ah, business . . .

☐ Here is *The PPP* cost-out, so you can see where the money goes. Of the total $14,500 expenses, we had to invest about a third up-front. The rest will be generated from sales. La. For budgeting your own book, you may want to use these five cost-categories as a checklist. However, your dollar figures are sure to swing wildly from ours. These will depend on your book's unique size, number of pages, paper stock, press-run, the form of distribution used, how much work you job out to other people at what rate, how much you budget for promotion, etc.

Our figures are based on promoting and selling 4,500 books of our 5,000 press-run; 500 copies are give-aways for reviews and passionate "patrons" of Booklegger. Break-even will be after 2,900 copies are sold. Alleluia! Then to keep on keeping on, we need continuing sales "profit" to stake the next bonanza. If we sell the whole run, we'd have around $8,000 to take another ride. Somewhere.

PLANT COST = $3,500. This is the one-time-only cost incurred creating any book. It is the same whether you publish one copy or one million. This is the expense that can be written off if you have the pleasure of going into multiple printings. Ours included: Research, writing & editing fees ($2,500). Design, typesetting, & paste-up ($1000).

PRINTING = $4000. Text paper ($1,606); Cover paper ($633: fervid fuchsia was on sale, *i.e.*, "close-out." Tell your printer if you are the garage-sale type.) Printing charges ($1,261). Binding ($500).

MARKETING = $1,500. All the promotion functions used in getting a book exposed to its market. Ours will include mailing list rental, mailing piece costs, postage, ad space, free books for review & kisses, publicist labor costs.

DISTRIBUTION = $4,500. Most of our business is mail-order, rather than bookstore. Postage & supplies for shipping books ($2,000). Order processing labor at $3 per hour ($2,500).

OVERHEAD = $1,000. All "indirect" operating costs pro-rated per book, such as rent, utilities, office supplies, accounts management, general maintenance & gardening.